THE HUMBLING AND OTHER POEMS

Robert J. Tiess

Copyright © 2022 Robert J. Tiess

All rights reserved.

No part of this book may be reproduced, or stored in a retrieval system, or transmitted in any form or by any means, electronic, mechanical, photocopying, recording, or otherwise, without express written permission of the author.

Cover design by: Robert J. Tiess

Printed in the United States of America

+ *Dedication* +

*In loving memory
of my mother, Jeannette,*

and my father, Robert.

*Thank you both,
and God,
for everything.*

+

CONTENTS

Title Page	
Copyright	
Dedication	
== The Poems ==	1
I.	2
The Humbling	3
Amid the Jersey Turnpike Whales	5
Another Word for Love	6
Vicarium	7
Elsewhere in the Coffeehouse...	9
Florescence	10
Now I've Become a Butterfly	11
Stargazers on a Winter's Night	12
We Are Water	13
Trevi Fountain	14
Still Here	15
Butterfly Mindset	16
Obsidian with Sheens of Gold	17
II.	20
Attending the Poet	21
Conversations with Gaia	22
Phoenix: Salvation	23
In Perpetuity	24
Interior Kingdom	25
Unbound	27
Between these Leaves	28

A Raindrop on Its Journey	29
To a Praying Sculpture	31
On the Revolutions of Copernicus	33
Unfinished Portrait	34
Postcards from Utopia	36
Observatory	38
Vanishing Points of View	39
Remembrance of a Future's Past	40
Upgrade	41
The Unpaved Road	42
Lotus Dreamer	44
So It Goes	45
What Dreams May Leave	46
April, Autumnal	47
Phoenix: Eternal	48
III.	49
Hidden in Plain Sight	50
Spacewalk of Life	51
Time, Who Rules Them All	52
Wide Angle Lens	53
Vermeer's Astronomer	54
Deer Haven	55
All Hands on Deck	57
Underwater	58
To Tolkien, the Mythmaker	60
Amazed	62
Destinations	63
Uncommon Choreography	65

Valedictory	66
To a Chess Computer	67
Metatheater	68
Choral	69
In an Upstate of Mind	71
Metropolis	72
IV.	74
Art of Diversity	75
Credo	76
One Sculpture, Seven Spectators	78
Through the Lens of Love	80
Epitaph	81
Behold	83
The Halcyon Days	86
Abscission	87
Prayer for the Voices of Resistance	89
Revivify	91
The Phoenix Way	92
Gamut	93
V.	94
All at Once (Through a Time Traveler's Eyes)	95
Resurfacing	96
The Gravity Beyond Our Blame	97
Significant Other, Signifying	99
Out of the Labyrinth, into the Light	100
To a Ventriloquist	101
Cubist Dancers	103
Quantum Poetical	104

Renovation of a Soul	106
Limited or No Connectivity	107
To the Spirit of My Lion Father	108
The Tigress to Her Loving Cub	110
The War Within	111
Architects of the Impossible	112
VI.	113
Escaping Escapism	114
Tell Them the Whole Truth	115
The Hidden Optimists	119
Valuation	120
Rights of Passage	121
Personal Copernican Revolution	122
Necessary Separation	123
The Song of Walt Is Our Song	124
Pas de Deux	128
Transcending Dialectics	129
Inside Collapsing Mines of Hope	130
VII.	131
Withstanding	132
Unfinished Symphony	133
Sacred Flight	134
Tao	135
Love's Special Relativity	136
Valediction	137
Building the Ark of Love	139
Lodestars	141
The Art of Rock Balancing	142

Dreaming Beyond Stairways	143
All in Their Times	145
Deepmost	147
Emblazon	148
Soul Windows	149
Semester's End at Raphael's School of Athens	150
AfterPoem	151
Toward Wisdom from Humility	152
= Addenda =	153
About Me	154
My "Eleven M's of Poetry"	162
=== Three Brief Essays ===	166
Essay I: Humility & Socrates	167
Essay II: The Vicarium	173
Essay III: Accessible Me	176
Poetry Words: A Very Brief Glossary	183
Some Poetry Reading Suggestions	190
Some Books About Poetry	191
Some Poets You Might Like	193
Additional Poets You Might Consider	195
Some Poetry Publications	202
Websites	203
Acknowledgements	205

= Welcome =

Greetings, friend, to my debut poetry collection. I'm honored and grateful you can join me here.

Unified by the theme of humility, these poems represent various stages of a larger journey toward freedom, compassion, selflessness, understanding, wisdom, bliss, and peace.

While this collection has been arranged in seven parts, its poems can be read in any order, from cover to cover, randomly, or any other way you wish.

Wherever you begin, I hope something in these leaves gives you joy.

After my poems, I provide some optional reading material about me, some of my ideas, and poetry itself.

Thank you for reading my book.

With much appreciation and love,

Robert

== **THE POEMS** ==

I.

Past vanity,
I climb to see...

THE HUMBLING

I love the world that humbled me
along my march toward 33,

a time so prime, profuse with pride,
when confidence intensified

and knowledge lead me to exalt
my educations to a fault.

In truth, I had to learn much more
than anything I read before,

experiences still to gain,
mistakes to make, the novel pain

of giving up some foolish dream
then tread the edge of self-esteem

and reckon with the emptiness,
where suppositions evanesce.

I took such pleasure in a fact,
the trivia I could extract,

my theories of the cosmic ways
among those bold, conceited days.

I'm just a student, one who sees
the paradox of Socrates,

to understand I do not know,
and yet enlighten as I go

to question things (myself as well),
mull modestly, and rarely dwell

at any point of prominence.

ROBERT J TIESS

No humbled heart wants dominance.

AMID THE JERSEY TURNPIKE WHALES

Two tractor trailers blow by fast
and drench my windows with their mist.

My hatchback's one slick dolphin here,
though small and gray among those whales.

The highway has become our sea
inhabited by sharks and eels

which weave between great waves of rain
and schools of luminescent cars

whose red and yellow spotlights glow
before the coral blur of trees.

Another trailer splashes through,
accompanied by pilot cars.

I eye my exit, nearly fishtail
flailing homeward one more time

in search of smoother waters yet,
no loggerheads, no snaring net,

just shallow couch, some songs that flow,
the lure of light and life I know,

and bubbles in my bath or glass,
as dreams, like ships I captain, pass.

ANOTHER WORD FOR LOVE

We breathe the word so frequently
I hope it ever resonates
like bells in my cathedral heart
whenever our feelings wed.

I've mentioned *treasure*, *cherish*, *doting*,
fond, *admire*, and *desire*,
prize, *adore*, *amour*, and more,
but what can mean as much as *love*?

The thesaurus lends no advice.
Inventive terms might well suffice,
until we use all those up, too.
Perhaps I won't state *I love you*.

Instead, I'd show it every day.
My actions speak. Hear what they say.

VICARIUM

A stranger in your house of thoughts,
I dwell in your experiences,
walk your halls and spiral stairs
to rummage through your sundry rooms
with shock or curiosity.

I rove in hopes to sense your mind
in anything you left behind:
the roll-top desk now halfway jammed,
a calendar extinct for years,
one musty mix of memories:

the phonograph (no vinyl near),
a toppled urn, white butterflies.
And, while I stare, I realize
such artifacts betray few hints
like pottery or art dug up

by guessing archaeologists
who trace unknowns with wary hands,
expecting to detect an edge
of fact instead of shattered myth
they'd try to reconstruct in time.

From here I cannot grasp your rhyme,
your nature, hatred, loves, or heart,
much less your science, song, or art.
I must be you and not your things,
espouse your atoms to the last,

absorb your stories, live your past,
breathe in your voice, dismiss myself,
endure your scars, your every choice,

envelop nothing but the whole
if I presume to know your soul.

ELSEWHERE IN THE COFFEEHOUSE...

Behind the bankers
    praising gains,

a critic picking
    at his stew,

and theorists
    thrashing formulas,

a former waitress
    sips her chai

    then calmly writes
        new verses which

        will save a life
            someday.

FLORESCENCE

Let aspirations reach as leaves
which feel for sun beyond the clouds,

whatever warmth and radiance
might make your mind more like the rose:

    soft petals flaring
glorious

    revealing richness
waking art,

    geometries
outside all lines

        poised high
    upon a sturdy stem
        encompassing important thorns

        so no one thieves too easily
    or ruins blooms ahead of time
before those blossoms burst with truth.

Your dreams must not be mere bouquets
which prettify but wither soon.

Embrace the sky, its grace and light!
Unfurl and thrive! Be bold and bright!

NOW I'VE BECOME A BUTTERFLY

The past no longer limits me.
I drift on wind and live as free

above the houses, mountains, clouds,
the cities gripped by anxious crowds,

alighting where I will by day
whenever I decide to stay.

You find me fragile, mock my might,
but can you lift yourself in flight?

Some dub me inessential, small,
but my effects affect us all

as I exert these tiny wings
and set in motion larger things.

If you should hear me, let me teach
that transformation's in your reach:

you could turn into something more,
become a living metaphor,

inspire others to aspire
to beauty, truth, existence higher

than empty notions left behind
once thoughts can soar beyond the mind.

STARGAZERS ON A WINTER'S NIGHT

With lowered scarves and gaping mouths,
we sigh with awe as starlight gleams
as crystalline as arctic snow.
Small homes below with Christmas lights
establish pleasant symmetries
between the valley and the sky.

A dog calls out to Sirius
(I let myself imagine here)
perhaps to wish its mate goodnight.

With one glove off, you trace the heavens,
fingers full of reverence,
which point out constellations you
identify by common names
– the dragon, swan, a lion, bears –
much like an evening at the zoo
except these creatures run forever
through the cosmic wilderness.

I see the whale from head to tail,
its fins held wide while it will breach
the ocean's darkness with such grace
that nothing splashes back to earth
to snuff our modest makeshift fire
as it dives down around our campsites
at the height of evergreens,

the universe and us beheld
at once within its giant eyes
before it swims around, compelled
to hurry upward toward the skies.

WE ARE WATER

Your current turns my water wheel,
drives my heart's machinery.

I am the water for your brush,
a part of all the art you paint.

Your waters bear me as I sail
throughout your world in search of love.

I'm strong as ice when you decide
to figure skate across my thoughts.

You baptize me, admit my soul
into your heaven, where I'm whole.

We thirst for life and flow as one:
this blissful river we become.

TREVI FOUNTAIN

Grandeur grips, then columns bolster
majesty most mythical:

Corinthian-rich symmetries
cresting in triumphal arches

charged upon by chariots
as Oceanus oversees,

new tempests welling in his waves
while heaving steeds rear up to lunge

and Tritons tensely rein them in
this raging frame of ancient pomp

where tourists pour to photograph
or plunder purses, pockets, pants,

obliged to clutch at least three coins
and sling them into whirlpool dreams.

STILL HERE

Let earthquakes
        rage
     and rivers
          rush,
volcanoes
       blaze
     and comets
          crush.
Let stars
      – all time –
         go
            disappear.
My
love
for
you
would
still
be
here.

BUTTERFLY MINDSET

        I crawled too far
     through dirt

and hurt

to disregard
this urgency

     to overgrow
         all former selves

            alight my spirit
            on new winds

   with weightless wings

pure buoyancy

to soar me there
where I could
be:

   among the blossoms
   brilliantly.

OBSIDIAN WITH SHEENS OF GOLD

I excavate cerebral strata

superseded sentiments

abandoned answers buried by
bold questions like Vesuvius
erupting until covering
all corners of my Pompeii mind.

I comb through rubble, relics, rot
excavating artifacts

the toppled columns of conjectures

glassy shards of hard beliefs

worn cornerstones of calculations

decaying reasons in debris.

Collapsed foundations clog the soil:

how groundlessly I used to toil
querying and quarrying

constructing wonders
stages

walls

between the secret and the shown
or what it was I should have known.

This province of my ignorance
ran further than I recollect

(a legacy of retrospect
nobody could bestow but me).

The world felt compact in my hands;

so little I had grasped
back then.

In any inch seek history:

gnarled trees of logic I dare scaled

each branch expressive of division
splitting into strange conditions

motley leaves of contradictions

vague silhouettes of inclinations

captivating vacillations

riven limbs to revelations
rarely fathomed
up or down

beyond the arches of conceit
felled by theories
incomplete

enigmas weathered
to no edge

the implications past the hedge.

I climb above a crumbling ledge,
survey my bygone realm of myth

my fabricated Camelot

sword ascending

me pretending
to be him, the fabled knight
whose asking spares the wounded king
and saves the wasteland from its plight.

Or I played Faust
infernal fool
who barters his eternity
for knowledge wrought of vanity.

Promethean
I sought to be
endowing the creative flame
necessitating sacrifice,

if only one
may pay that price.

Odysseus, another name:
he's partly me, I tend to think
absorbed by stories,
oceans, and time,
yet persevering in return
to only what will matter most:

fidelity and love divine.

Each contemplative odyssey
delivers me near intersections:

new truths crisscrossing old deceptions

futurities
antiquities

my shadows angled at the night.

There's graduation from the ruins

small degrees
toward dawning sight:

more golden mornings born of light!

II.
...beyond the country of myself...

ATTENDING THE POET

Despite distorted microphones,
the whooshing traffic, playground fray,
the smartphone taps, and hallway chats,

a poet speaks above the fuss
to those attending to attend

– who know they need to heed those words.

CONVERSATIONS WITH GAIA

Beyond the rambling waterfalls,
the thunders mumbling in their sleep,
and crickets with encrypting trills,
the dialogues run far and deep
throughout the forests most ignore:

the histories of all that crawls,
with whispers (why do willows weep?)
the drawing claw, a beak that drills,
those vultures that descend to reap,
the valley echoes full of lore.

Hear howling wolves and yowling prey
repeatedly beseech each night
as bats ask past the voice of light
and owls sound new inquiries
while whales sing under silent seas.

Mind what the rising rivers say,
the tidings of the geese in flight,
the mountain peaks no longer white,
how climates speak between degrees.
Let's learn the language of the trees!

PHOENIX: SALVATION

There will be those who weigh you down
or lure you lower than
the ground.

Around the crater of your crash
they'll sift through cinders,
comb for bones

or gamble you'd be gone for good,
supposing none survive
such falls.

Confer protection, brilliance, warmth.
Exhausting thoughts, be love
and burn

though they'll know not what they have done:
forgive them quickly,
pray they learn.

Dust off the soot of loss and lean
toward honor, truth, and peace,
then leap!

How shocked they'll be to see you fly
beyond horizons
fears deny.

Be more than symbol, strength, and dream.
Be light! Inspire! Revive!
Redeem!

IN PERPETUITY

Too many years I thought this way,
concerning birth and history:
as someone I was yesterday
approaching who I'd choose to be.

We're every moment in our lives
– all instants, hours, years combined –
although our atoms, born of stars,
raise questions, like the soul and mind.

Are we not timeless, in some sense,
exceeding mere chronology?
We cannot live forever, yet
we touch upon eternity:

our mortal segments mark the line
that's measureless – infinity.
What was and is and must become
remains in perpetuity.

What this might mean, I cannot say,
except we're part of something vast.
Perhaps we should look well beyond
the future, present, and the past

to contemplate our cosmic source,
its transience and genesis,
existence in this ageless course,
the consequence of endlessness...

INTERIOR KINGDOM

One lie might eye the highest throne
inside the castle of your mind,
and any whim may play the lord
when left unchecked, out of control,
once knights of reason flee their posts,
let sentiments invade these walls,
then leave the keep without defense.
How easily a kingdom falls!

Observe horizons, what they bring,
which speculations stray too near,
impostor doctrines, daydreams, doubts,
especially that old foe, fear,
who preys upon all certainty
and sows misgivings everywhere.
Seek wisdom's counsel in a quest.
Receive the real. Stay aware!

Now, if your queen is empathy
and governs with a charity,
regarding others with esteem,
a peace might prosper through this realm,
one founded on her golden rule
to render what the self has sought
and cultivate much clarity
for many questions lost in thought.

Consider what your subjects say,
the banners you parade today,
the verse or voids within a voice,
your greatest treasures, every choice,
the bridge you lower or you lift
when strangers come to bear a gift.
Have Truth, your shield, close in hand,

and guard this most majestic land!

UNBOUND

Above Earth, evenings vanish fast
    while I'm in orbit, floating slow.

Each planetary revolution
    sparks from darkness without war,

transitions into silent peace
    between extremes of dusk and dawn.

Illumination, ageless space:
    here, shadows cannot subdue worlds.

The stars, once born in beds of dust,
    expect to lend the void their light.

The universe may seem like night,
    but nothing there pronounces hours

or vouches time had any powers
    over this eternity,

to score it all in mortal ticks
    then govern with inconstancy.

Again, as twilight veers around,
    such endlessness remains unbound,
        and everything exists as free.

BETWEEN THESE LEAVES

No, life's not wholly vanished here.
You only have to look for it,
behind, before, between these leaves,
above the broken ends of branches
where one small bluebird takes its pause
and, higher up, two crows await
more flocks of darkness, which must come,
(like death, for some, but not to me)
to take the place of foliage
and caw the forest from its wake
until a flurry turns to whiteout
and winter seems to clean the slate
entirely, but not quite so:

for even then there shall be birds,
an evergreen not far away,
fresh berries barely visible,
the flashing reds of cardinals,
a wispy chimney up the road,
the plotting fox beneath a bush,
the stationary snowshoe rabbit,
a den of bear cubs fast asleep,
the frosty brook where deer appear,
take quiet sips, wait out the night,
then leave few hints they lingered there
where we regain the covered trail,
our surest steps obscured by wind,
and so few clues we passed this place.

A RAINDROP ON ITS JOURNEY

Through water cycles, year by year,
I fall, ascend, and soon appear

upon a bride in summer rain
or on the groom who waits in vain;

on knights in quest of victories
or captains trapped in angry seas;

upon the critics which commend
or farmers pleading droughts to end;

on top of tears already cried
or in the eyes of shattered pride;

upon the maiden on her mare
or servants bursting from despair;

on new musicians chasing sound
or climbers finding higher ground;

upon the poets dazed with pages
or dramatists who dream of stages;

on saints and sinners, fools or kings
or mermaids swimming as they sing;

upon the builders heaving stones
or diggers dusting ancient bones;

on artists starting on a scene,
or seekers of the unforeseen;

upon astronomers at night
or lovers reaching for the light;

on astronauts returned to Earth

or mothers running to give birth;

upon philosophers and knaves
or grievers weaving through the graves.

Descending to evaporate,
I rise again, embrace my fate.

Perhaps in time, I'll land on you
and see life from your point of view.

TO A PRAYING SCULPTURE

In deathless reservation,
poised

– perfecting silence –

cold,
composed

(hermetic eyelids,
steadfast lips
relenting never unto breath):

you plead across eternity,
requesting blessings,
knowledge,
strength

with fingers inextricable,
hardened,
godly in resolve.

I say you pray
for strangers, peace;

for absolution, love, defense;

for gratitude, more tolerance,
and guidance, patience, justice, truth;

for mysteries, a revelation
over fleshly contemplation.

Deprived of motion,
defect,
doubting,
nearly any transience,

you are the model of devotion,

faithfulness unwavering,

suggesting creed,
sublime designs,

the mind and life
become divine.

ON THE REVOLUTIONS OF COPERNICUS

Before you, universal Earth,
perfected cosmic centerpiece,
enduring rest, revolved by sun,
entrapped in egocentric terms
appropriating all creation.

And then your model, like a clock,
startled gears from slumbrous turns,
awakened pupils to the sun:
unorthodox astronomies
yet reverent in the mass of all.

You shattered axes of false worlds,
releasing them like whirligigs
away from rash initial twirls,
momentum gaining strength to slow
one vertigo of history:

how blazing revelations rise
though we grow cold to profound sights
and orbit blind in starless nights
until new truths set questions free.

UNFINISHED PORTRAIT

The canvas cannot capture me.
I'll rise before the painting dries.

No photograph snaps fast enough
to picture me beyond
a blur.

My life shall not be
paused like film:
constrained,
one image

stilled in frame,

too
closely
cropped

and stopped midway

between the person
I once was
and everything
I must become.

This also goes for verse or prose:
all epics are inadequate.
Biography's just summary,
abbreviated history,
superficial, incomplete.

What does come close to showing me?
Unfinished art, a symphony
whose restless music never ends
but scales outside the printed score.

Refuse to be diminished, friends!
No one was small! We're so much more!

POSTCARDS FROM UTOPIA

Old postcards from the antique shops
portraying places far from here,
in miles and in many years.

The old-time pictures, photos, ads,
locations unknown, almost flawless,
ever invitational:

vacations I might try someday,
attractions you have heard about,
most regions one will never reach.

These open notes penned on the back
will often wish that you were here
- the "you" not you, of course, and yet

it could be you - not you, right here -
but elsewhere in the multiverse,
where you dress very differently,

have varied tastes, another life,
and seek adventures overseas
or wish to wander on a whim,

or fall asleep in pricey inns
with heart-shaped pools and neon lights,
or maybe crave more ancient sights

- a castle, fortress, pyramid -
or relish benches by the lake,
or drive down roads no others take.

Perhaps you mend a shattered heart
and visit Greece, or Spain, or Rome
or some estate, another home

where someone stays the night, no more,
because too much is left to tour
before tomorrow's history.

Most postcards feel addressed to me,
and some include my given name.
And, here, they tell me, "Try this train,"

a classic one with puffs of steam
that chugs by mountains and a stream.
And now I'm in it, like a dream.

OBSERVATORY

My eyes adjusted to the darkness
on this crisp and cloudless night,
I tremble, tune my telescope,
in hopes of tracking Saturn's rings.

I call you quickly, but they're gone
before you close your robe and come.
I turn the dials one more time,
but it's too chilly, so you go.

How Earth is restless, like my wonder,
caught in orbit, bound by light,
revolving in some cosmic plan
astronomers might understand.

But this is curiosity,
a good excuse to breathe brisk air
before I turn the lamps back on
and read to sleep in my old chair.

I need no stars to explicate
the energy within our kiss.
To feel your heartbeat, grasp your hand,
or waltz with you is to understand

the galaxies and everything,
eternities disguised as time,
this multiverse of mystery:
your love's the lens that lets me see.

VANISHING POINTS OF VIEW

They're there along the longest roads,
where lines dividing either lane
converge on distant points of light
which never speak of left or right.

And they are in the railroad tracks
conducting luggage here to there
then disappearing far away
with the death or birth of day,

until you move, adjust the view
(perspectives trending where you stand)
and the old world starts to skew
as angles wrangle with the land,

and elsewhere, from some higher ground,
perhaps a lost thing can be found,
or what was hidden gets revealed:
the precipice becomes a field.

REMEMBRANCE OF A FUTURE'S PAST

The future gives a splendid speech
of promising tomorrows:
discoveries, new loves in reach,
yet nothing of the sorrows
of histories we have declined
to memorize or bear in mind.

We turn a page from yesterday,
ignoring what it had to say
because it can sound out of date
and not enough of us relate
to wisdoms ages may impart.
But this is where our follies start.

Hear prospects holler, "Look ahead,
beyond the elder and the dead!"
Then we'll pursue a further year
(which often comes across as near)
when we would prosper from the past,
collect its lessons, learn (and fast)

the future's roots grew long ago
before we knew to look behind
and fathom how all moments flow
outside of time if we could find
to look back is to have the chance
to see tomorrow and advance.

UPGRADE

I'm no computer, yet you did
discover ways to upgrade me,

increasing my capacity
to memorize, decode, and know

while moving forward with a drive
to process and accept it all

with chipless shoulders strong enough
to take upon the daily loads.

Enduring, storing, still belonging,
no longer feeling obsolete,

at last, my data has a base,
and every bit falls into place.

I sense the errors in my source
where questions pressed with dumb brute force

in fatal loops to "solve for x"
until you sighed and I'd perplex.

The world seems stable, able, clear,
when we connect with love, my dear.

Your input fixed my crashing heart.
Because of you, my life can start.

THE UNPAVED ROAD

The Unpaved Road
Unevenly, that's me. I go
careening left or right or low
above rough hills or mountaintops
by rivers, timber, sudden drops,
and, if it rains, I turn to mud
and laugh when wheels spin and scud.

No signs to speak of, fancy rails,
or lights at night, just winding trails,
to roam however long I like.
I'm often crossed on foot or bike.

Most city cars get lost out here,
beside the squirrels, beavers, deer,
and rush on through before the dark
demands they slow down or they park,
endure an evening without sleep
as owls screech and shadows leap
beneath a moon waxed ghostly white
while silhouettes slip out of sight.

Yes, other roads run well-behaved,
but that's their tough luck, being paved.
Out here I'm careless as the land,
and no one needs to understand
why I prefer to rove so coarse,
or why my closest friend's a horse,
or why I must not be refined,
or how it is I'm so resigned
to lend no sense of here or there
and might as well lead anywhere

except the place you'd rather be.
I go my way, with nature, free.

LOTUS DREAMER

Plunged under mud,
    oblivious,

beneath the surface
    of a world,

you wonder
    when you start to rise,

if light exists
    outside this night,

but this is how
    it all begins:

from darkness
not of any sins

    then growth
    and
    blooming into grace

toward beauty's truth:
your sacred space.

SO IT GOES

Upon this bridge of stalwart stone
I sense enduring steadiness,

the sureness of eternity
that knows no ending
nor beginning.

The reeling stream serves turbulence,
an everlasting restlessness
which illustrates the rush of time

from past,
through present,
flooding futures.

I'll pause midway to mind the flow
and then advance, as all must go.

WHAT DREAMS MAY LEAVE

To live
>or not to live:

>*never the question!*

But awakening from
this slumberous existence

>unto undiscovered truths

must give us mortals
cause.

APRIL, AUTUMNAL

The mottled leaves of memories descend
from nervous forests in her trembling mind
as if a sleeping winter might awake
before her world should wholly resurrect.

Then withered minutes slip from listing limbs:
a birthday missed, an anniversary,
the January calendar unchanged,
a mislaid face, some misplaced name or year.

Old foliage ignores the anxious sun
since dismal winds convince each brittle branch
to hold no moment closely or too long
now shadows spread and all turns silhouette.

But then she smiles, reviving life with light,
and hope may spring eternal one more night.

PHOENIX: ETERNAL

When death's no end, how does one spend
the countless lives which lie ahead?

What comes of such eternity
if all I am is merely me?

I sense new purpose must be found
in each beginning coming round:

to not repeat what went before,
but rather become something more

than death and life made to repeat
or progress lost with each retreat.

I should grow stronger with each fall,
retain some wisdom after all,

fly higher, further, which each burn,
and from my ashes always learn.

Perfection being God's alone,
yet there are truths I could have known

and many things I should refine
before the next time I resign.

When resurrecting, may I free
myself from what I used to be

and elevate in every way,
in body, mind, and soul each day.

III.
...a frontier rich
with revelations...

HIDDEN IN PLAIN SIGHT

Most secrets of the universe
stand up before our very eyes
and wave with both hands every day
in hopes someone may look their way.

But few among us lean to see
so closely as to realize
those meanings leaping from each leaf
or where a stone provokes belief,

or how the howling mountain sings,
or why these trees wear many rings,
what fireflies imply tonight,
or whom the moon cues with its light.

More curious we'll need to be
to simply listen to the sea,
attend the rivers' poetry,
and savor nature's symphony.

The declarations signed by stars,
the caveats of Venus, Mars,
the wisdom which a prism gives,
the histories of all that lives,

the eloquence of butterflies,
the social ants that colonize,
the octopus embracing change,
and crystal atoms that arrange:

bold messages sent everywhere
with tempting questions, if we dare
to sit beside a fading rose
and humbly ask it what it knows.

SPACEWALK OF LIFE

Umbilical

with Mother Earth

    (oceans
    flowing
    amniotic)

I'm meditating

    childbirth

    constellations

    every nation

    deliverance

    new unity:

our universal family.

TIME, WHO RULES THEM ALL

Before it, kings must genuflect,
and heads of states shall pay respect.
Queens will curtsy, troops salute,
and legislators constitute.

For this is Time, Who Rules Them All,
commanding suns to jump and fall
then clocking moons around for weeks
and seizing hours when it speaks,

whole days in deadly decrements.
Time calibrates our instruments,
grips histories within ghostly hands,
and shackles wrists within its bands.

Invincibly, upon its throne,
Time reigns supreme, from stars to stone.
But stare there, longer, without fear,
and find what truth might soon appear:

the crown's as empty as that chair!
Now, where's our master, if not there?
Invention? Merely measurement
with no domain or government

controlling moments we will cede?
To understand is to be freed.

WIDE ANGLE LENS

At first, I see the scenes through me
refract in ego's glassy walls

(pure light furled into selfish bands,
the icy edges of those panes

dividing up my muddled sight
in facets of vague vanity)

– but then I blink, begin to think
of anything outside my lens,

what waits beyond my inward eyes,
and once again I realize

how little senses have perceived,
what clarity could be received

if I would focus further still,
exploring broader panoramas

–mountains, valleys, rivers, lakes,
the skyline where a new day breaks,

the unknown moments, hours, years,
untraveled miles and frontiers–

and contemplate a greater view
until I learn the world, and you.

VERMEER'S ASTRONOMER

Celestial, the globe you turn,
the microcosm in your hand,
each star imparting worlds to learn,
mechanics you must understand.

Copernicus once leaned like you,
found revolutions in the spheres,
then calculated planets, too,
and now you search for finer gears,

why constellations circulate,
and how a comet loops through skies,
notating angles, mass, and rate,
elusive clues before your eyes.

At times, you almost have it right
until some figure fails to fit.
You map from morning into night,
as far the cosmos will permit.

A theory sets you on a path.
You sense there's more than mortal math.
The universe propels past cause,
and thus, you wonder, and you pause.

DEER HAVEN

Now that the plowman's driven off,
nine deer edge back with gentle steps
through thickets caked with heavy snow,
returning to their favorite acres.

They wander round the fenceless yard,
will stiffen at the slightest hint
of hikers slogging down the trail.
Serene yet ever vigilant.

One doe folds up her legs and yawns
while her fawns frolic, swerve, and leap,
imprinting patterns, figure eights,
expending restless energies.

An antlered deer's near motionless
as he regards the larger scene.
Apart from instinct, I suspect
experiences schooled him well,

how precious moments meant a life
around the woods old hunters roamed
or perched on branches patiently
until a quarry crawled too close.

The wind which leaves us trembling,
that's nothing to deter the deer.
One frigid gust and in we'll dash
toward fireplaces, quilts, or tea.

These deer abide, sit out a squall,
face elements with fortitude,
then weather winters into springs.
I praise their ways. They teach me things

like welcoming whatever is,
to stride in peace, eat just enough,
respecting earth, its menaces,
prioritizing family

despite those fields lost each year
since commerce thrives where they once grazed.
The mountain slumps, demoted here
behind bold billboards crowding views.

Construction trucks rush on the hour,
deposit concrete, steel, pipes.
Some displaced deer bolt over here,
and more lay lost along the route.

I found why deer die in the light:
their eyes, dilated in the dark,
get flooded by the sudden glare.
So they stay sightless, wait and see.

You'd think by now they'd know to go.
I wish they had some sort of lore
to warn their kin of fiendish roads
and frame car beams as devil's eyes.

My meadows offer sanctuary,
a hideaway from urban sprawl.
Those deer are more than welcome here.
They're family. I love them all.

ALL HANDS ON DECK

Tumultuous, the ocean throws
a listing ship from wave to stew
where darkness swells and panic grows.
Then thunder stuns the shrunken crew.
They clutch at ropes or hopes and swear,
"The captain, he must get us there!"

- that island where they would retire
and share their tales beside the fire,
recounting swords that slashed at sails,
the cannonballs, the sharks and whales,
the pirates, mermaids undersea,
rare treasures lost to mutiny.

As lightning gives a glimpse of death,
the sailors gasp with famished breath
while water crashes bow and stern
and threatens wreckage should they turn
against the captain at this hour
- that stalwart soul, forever dour -

who helms the wheel, barks commands,
and summons all surviving hands
to save this ship, and fast, or leave.
They batten hatches, scramble, heave,
and stand united, through the night,
to not go down without a fight.

UNDERWATER

Beneath the surface
    I could see
        such hidden fish

        the whales

        debris

    which currents burgeon
        into waves

        old sunken ships

        the bony graves
    of all who perished
questing gold

        the octopus

    what maps withhold

the untold wonders

coral

lights
emerging from
    much deeper nights
than anything I've ever known

    concealed caves

    ruins unknown

    a sea of secrets so profound
my world views change
when I reach

ground.

TO TOLKIEN, THE MYTHMAKER

From ancient lore, lost lingual arts,
through verses birthed in precious flames,
you summoned heroes, wizards, fiends,
all archetypes of journeying,
with giants, tyrants, signs and songs,
enchanting realms with mighty tales
that bring us back where all begins:
in times benign with lesser sins,

a world serenely free, at ease,
before the gore and tortured trees,
mad shadows hounding after powers
as seething creatures curse the hours
of swarming armor, clashing swords,
the braying horses, raving hordes
of warriors called forth to slay
vast dragons crashing in the fray.

Your ringing legends resonate
past fantasy to fascinate
a seeker, dreamer, child, or sage
to wander off the beaten page
with purpose, nerve, perhaps a smile,
and stride outside a country mile
for fellowship, adventure, light,
returning kings who'll set things right

so others may engage and dance,
revel or rest, reflect, romance,
know innocence and purity,
tranquility, security,
until some evil rears its head,

fresh demons feed upon old dread,
new champions ascend to fight
and come full circle in this rite.

AMAZED

You place me somewhere in your maze
then watch me wander merrily,
directionless and tentative,
inquisitive with any turn,
until I trace my every step
and rove past walls I saw before.

From where you stand, I look confused,
so indecisive, helpless, done.
But I'm not searching how to leave
this pleasant realm of mystery.
I relish being lost in here,
meandering through who you are,

exploring more untraveled paths
that take me closer toward your core:
the secret entrance of your soul.
Sometimes I fear I'll stray too near
by truths perhaps you hope none find
and you might move me yet again.

A mouse would solve this handily,
except I like to probe unknowns
and be amazed by what I find
along the corners of your mind.
Wherever you will let me start,
l love to learn your ways by heart.

DESTINATIONS

Tomorrows hinge
    on one decision.

In all directions:
    consequence.

Momentum dwells
    in every step,

progressions trending
    backward, forth,

some bending by
    a point of peace

or heading for a
    wasteland plagued.

Degrees of causes
    finely drive

effects toward unknown
    destinations:

one smidgen off
    may lead near love

        or veer into
    new desolation

or end someplace
    no one expects

beyond the road
    no hope selects.

To do, remain,

ROBERT J TIESS

be still, or voice:

such influence
in one small choice!

Those futures you
would gain or lose

commence, right here,
with what you choose.

UNCOMMON CHOREOGRAPHY

We never dance as others do
    when silence dies
        then heartbeats rise
and music breathes me into you

love's torrid song
    sung by our eyes

      reviving wild rhapsody

yet harmony

    ballet of souls

all motions flowing beautifully:

    what no one tempers
    or controls.

Yes, we must whirl
    imperfectly

in steps we take
    where we desire

acutely true
      intensely free

    barefooted through
      both ice and fire.

VALEDICTORY

No new diplomas
to unroll

or mortarboards

(or lofty speech
assuring dreamers
they may reach)

just failed exams

electives dropped

professors lost

commencements stopped

when no one stands to graduate
from histories which illustrate
some course of action in reverse
creates a crisis even worse
than any text or test would cover.

At any moment we'd discover
curriculum looms everywhere,
beyond the blackboard, desk, and chair,
if we admit humility
should be our university
whose faculty includes the past,
experiences small and vast,
mistakes, with failure as the dean,
degrees conferred by what we'd glean.

Alumni of antiquities,
let's educate futurities.

TO A CHESS COMPUTER

You calculate a billion plays
(within the space I take a breath)

and mostly have it figured out
where both my knights will meet their death

before they have a chance to ride
into the battle you had won

just as our game gets underway.
I've hardly started, and you're done!

You recognize all openings,
the strategies of centuries.

This could be even if I would
command as many memories.

You're like Goliath, yes, my friend,
a giant getting in my way.

I'll never be as strong or tall,
although I learn more every day.

Last week I checked you twice but lost.
Perhaps next month it might be mate.

My name is David, by the way.
That's either funny or that's fate.

METATHEATER

Wide eyes attend each fleeting scene
enacted on that stage of sight,
where dramas clamor to be seen
until they exit, left or right.

Theatrics, every precious bit,
but look, when curtains rise,
how much of this we never see:
the backdrops, props, and guise.

Beyond these walls, so many roles
and plots advance the one true play:
protagonists we never met
in fateful settings far away,

old adversaries, vanquished myths,
faint scripts in tongues no longer read,
those ageless lines time casts away,
yet archetypes exempt from death.

No audience of senses know
the depth and length of every show,
much less the author of it all
or if there comes a curtain call.

Applaud the little we perceive,
and, as you do this, please believe
the fullest truth exceeds our views
while we wait for our lights and cues.

CHORAL

A would-be voice
draws shallow
breaths

from
lungs wrung void
of oxygen.

How can I sing
if you can't breathe?

Will we escape
these tainted airs,

the fumes and flames
of enmity,

step from the smog
of agony,

inhale pure peace
from mountaintops,

revive our sight,

significance,

the unity which once was ours?

Know: silence cannot be a power.

Gather.

Chant
in one vast voice
reverberating this:

our choice

to be heard
past the manic roars
of lies,
of hatred,
chaos,
wars.

Let's never fail to be so bold
to hear our truths and have them told!

IN AN UPSTATE OF MIND

More traffic jams and stunted turns:
the rustic in me often yearns
to leave behind this urban maze,
these concrete halls, the hectic haze,
and reach a route that curves away
across the bridges, burbs, and bay,
the smog and streets bogged in the fray
of someone always running late
and life at such a breakneck rate.

And so, it's settled: at this light,
I must drive left instead of right:
this leads me north, whence I was born,
among the horses, wheat, and corn,
where only mountains scrape the skies
and greener fields fill the eyes
with wildflowers, dragonflies
– whole acres no one tread before,
except the cattle, deer, or boar.

I have a certain spot in mind,
the opposite of grime and grind:
a lake to clear my weary head
and spare my soul from going dead
so I can lean back, recollect,
imagine, question, and reflect
on prospects, wishes, things to see,
then breathe, release, and simply be
as nature soothes and sets me free.

METROPOLIS

Shake off your fog,
our city.

Rise.

Ten thousand windows
mark your eyes:

come trace the raving traffic flow
as buses, cars, and taxis go
with subways, choppers, boats, and planes
across your routes like blood through veins
while scattered walkers gather, pace
before the concrete of your face.

Your shadows wax now you've grown tall,
and few can curb your urban sprawl,

assess your mettle, seize your soul,
appraise your arts, survey the whole,
or sift your music from the noise,
or penetrate your stoic poise,
or calm your reeling pulse at night,
or see beyond your neon light.

Metropolis,
I've heard you
breathe,

your weeping,
sighs.

You scream
and seethe.

You're more
than mortar,
blocks,
or height.

May all
your stories
lend us
sight.

IV.
...interpretations, further views...

ART OF DIVERSITY

The art exhibit helps us see
how much we need diversity:

the sundry brushwork, angles, hues,
perspectives framing varied views,

the untold styles one might find
as subjects run from mind to mind.

How specially each work portrays
a common thing in striking ways

or offers a familiar scene
to manifest the unforeseen

between the abstract and concrete.
No works alike, yet none compete

because the canvas fits it all
and makes a window of a wall,

a doorway through a stranger's face,
or course across some time or space,

where worlds and wonders stun, surprise,
and plead we see beyond our eyes

the individuality
essential to all artistry.

CREDO

Uncertainty assures me so
I've come to trust in doubtfulness

– the questioning of every thing –

advising judgements not to jump
into a chasm of untruth
where feelings balk at parachutes.

If sound convictions will not speak
when interviewed by scrutiny
(or only answer mystery)
let hesitations testify.

Inconstancy shall mean to me
all mortal creed outside of God.

And yet we can reach new beliefs
from winding paths, through wilderness,
the thinning mists of innocence,
the stubborn smog of ignorance,
all strange terrain and lands renamed,
inspiring souls to know a way
beyond what we were sold or told
or what a fact forgets to say.

Despite my blindness, faith could see
above these walls surrounding me
or walk with reason through these lands
which no persuasion understands
without adventure, sin, ordeal:

your self-reliance should be real!

Dear seeker, may we never find

the motive to enclose a mind
or only go by what some heard
between the bedlam and a bird.

Devotion cannot be a word.

With wonder, let's embrace our night,
yet pray we wake with inner light!

ONE SCULPTURE, SEVEN SPECTATORS

I.

Admonishing all mortal shells
which
thinning
peel

baring bone:

marrow at the cavities
not outliving skin or stone.

II.

A dream a seashell might have had
perhaps an oyster
yearning pearls
and opalescence of the dusk
it hears about
but never sees.

III.

An evolution of a theory
which began as basic math
sketched on napkins over lunch:
new formulas for gravity
explaining what we should have known.

IV.

What it feels like
to be crushed

by the weight
of clarity
if everything
was wrought of glass.

V.

The mountain's heart,
tough atrium:

pumping rigor
rhythm

life

throughout the bodies
of the world.

VI.

What you would see
if time could
freeze.

VII.

The months we moseyed
by the beach
where sand was fine
and waves were wide
and summertime
should never end.

THROUGH THE LENS OF LOVE

We've focused fondly,
eyes to sighs,

while crowds around us
blurred away.

Now, through love's lens,
we realize

(beyond the sharpness
of the fray)

what waits outside
of optics, sense,

and circles of
confusing light,

where timelessness
dissolves all tense:

eternal truths,
divine insight,

as everything
zooms into view

– potentials through
the multiverse,

from quarks and stars
to worlds diverse.

There, we are cosmic,
love come true.

EPITAPH

With sails propelled
by angel breath,
we'll glide outside
of life and death,
bequeath our time
and light to stars,
then leave behind
what once was ours.

Who brings such things
past heaven's gate?
So little will
perpetuate.
Although, consider
what was spent:
possessions,
decorations, rent,

those hours lost
to nervous strife,
the discontent
of spendthrift life,
when all we needed
wasn't much:

some shelter, food,
a loving touch

and dreams to give
the nights delight,

some hope to keep
the mornings bright,

then good to tell
a wrong from right,

with questions lending
fresh insight.

Until that ship
arrives, let's live,

revel, explore,
excite, and give

our hearts a chance
to love and laugh

so "joy" may be
our epitaph.

BEHOLD

There are such places
I might stand

to muse on beauty,
life unplanned,

and witness districts
small or wide,

where all belongs
beyond divide.

The vistas glisten.
Earth inspires.

Horizons bathe me
in their fires,

and often I'm
reborn up there

on mountaintops,
the open air.

I'll glimpse an eagle,
hawk, or crow

(which one it could be,
I don't know):

it soars and circles,
tilts, and fades

through cyan skies
as light cascades

while forests slip
from morning mist,

revealing what
worn eyes have missed

when farms and harvests,
cows and deer,

stand closer than
they first appear.

I'll go, return,
and work for days,

renewed, attuned
to life's own ways:

the gentle grandeur
of the green,

how flowers reach
and maples lean

by hillsides dipping
down to roll

without resistance,
fear, control,

and clouds that cluster,
bust, and fade

beside the corn
before the glade.

I pray you find
a spot as sweet

to meditate,

feel more complete,

then breathe until
you decompress

and savor nature,
free of stress

– how nature, I think,
means to be:

above contrivance,
ample, free,

instinctive, true,
serene though bold

with endless wonders
to behold.

THE HALCYON DAYS

Unflustered epoch, warmer, bright,
when all the world willed pure delight
and games gave chase through afternoons
on cloudless days in Mays or Junes:

then, time stood furthest from the mind
and spring was always close behind
wherever winter served its worst.
How we would hurry, sing, or burst

into the yards, play hide or seek,
watch butterflies, or climb to peek
beyond the forest full of thrills
to glimpse the mountain past the hills.

We swore we would explore it all,
run higher, deeper, like the ball
one throws much further thanks to age.
Impatiently we turned that page

and scurried toward maturity,
oblivious to misery.
The vernal hours vanish fast.
To those yet youthful: make them last!

ABSCISSION

One by
> one,
>> I drop
> them
> off

> like leaves
> upon
>> the autumn
> wind

> then watch
> them

> drift
> away
> and fade:

> those thoughts
> one must
> give up

> to live...

dejection, dreading,
anger, hurt

> confusion, sorrows,
> greed, regrets

anxiety
in any form

> nostalgia, bias,

       ignorance

suspicions, envy,
obsessions

       outmoded views,
       illusions, pride.

And, once it's done,
the branches of my mind are free
       to reach up toward
       the winter sky
       and grasp
       the
       cooler winds
       without
       the burdens
       of
the worrisome.

PRAYER FOR THE VOICES OF RESISTANCE

May words and purpose ride their horses,
rally truths, discover courses
into minds deceptions fenced,
where blind denial stands against
those notions that would disagree
with visions it pretends to see.

Let wisdom's lantern light the way
from cautious thought to what deeds say
so messages can echo clear
and facts, not factions, move you nearer
toward that realm where reason speaks
through valleys, cities, mountain peaks

and resonates across the land,
that anyone might understand
these tidings must pertain to all,
and, should you falter, more may fall
if history repeats once more
and justice suffers as before.

May peace be ever in your sight
and conquer hearts of those who'd fight
for false beliefs or grievous wrongs
or threaten hate where hope belongs.
Let patience be your secret shield
within that vicious battlefield.

May tolerance, in time, persuade
as old agendas bend and fade
till bold compassions come at last
to lift us from the tortured past

ROBERT J TIESS

toward futures where democracy
means justice loves equality.

REVIVIFY

More senses cloud and swell with storms:
impending lightning, wind, and floods

may saturate this arid span.
I pray the rain of life revives

the parched and hardened thoughts long scorched
by droughts of wonder, mirth, and zest.

– that vital clay, now cracked and pale,
once welcoming the wildflowers,

hummingbirds and evergreens,
essential streams, such butterflies,

not fissured flatland choked by bones
of perished questions, skulls of dreams:

necropolis born of neglects
and nothing no one recollects.

Let old convictions soak and soften,
loosen up, get swept away,

removed from stasis, surged with purpose,

churned till fertile, healed, seeded,

sunned beneath more tranquil light.
Let's resurrect a mind tonight!

THE PHOENIX WAY

Where others dwell on my demise,
I'll cast my ashes
then arise.

As some prepare to eulogize,
I'll spread new wings
to their surprise.

Before the coldness quells my eyes,
my love lights up
those starless skies.

Despite defeatists who despise,
my song lives on
to energize.

When death descends to finalize,
I'll resurrect,
revitalize.

GAMUT

No pixelations,
8-bit art.

The resolution of my heart
exceeds electric exhibition,

desires finer definition

like watercolors
which must
f l o w

or oil paintings
setting
s
l
o
w

so every nuance saturates
that canvas where each life creates
its masterpiece of choices made:

those strokes of words
and deeds portrayed

outside the borders of a screen

where things unseen
subsist and mean

beyond a glassy lavish glow.

There's more to see, to show,
and know.

V.
*...the questions,
endless wonderment...*

ALL AT ONCE (THROUGH A TIME TRAVELER'S EYES)

The past stood not behind us then
but onward, where old futures loomed
before the prospects yet to be.
Anticipating history,

we could be passing being born,
experiencing innocence,
establishing our origins,
just watching clocks spin backward, stop

when hours cease to signify
or sum potential measurements,
like distance lived inside a life
or what's the place of any age.

Few findings hinge on stillness now:
unending presence pivotal,
the sole point to survive the truth
that time's designed to disappear

those moments one should name a space,
meander through remembrance
or speculate on prophecies.
The present centers everything:

who wasn't, what would never show,
why something is or must become.
Continuum. No days or nights.
At once, right here, all cause unites.

RESURFACING

Float
    upward

        fathoms
        into light

    regaining
    breath

reclaiming
sight.

Now wrecks
    or treasures
    have been found

    let feet
    revisit
solid ground.

Remember drowning.
Master swimming.

Transmigrate toward
    your new beginning.

THE GRAVITY BEYOND OUR BLAME

The universe absorbs our faults
although we are to blame again.

Another thing comes tumbling down,
and gravitation takes the fall.

A fence collapses.
Avalanches.
Mudslides plunge the land in muck.
A paradise becomes unmade.

We mourn and move in retrograde.

How should we reckon with descent?
With which excuse?
To what extent?

We prop our reasons with emotions,
heap more feelings, straining sense,
then seem surprised when just an ounce
of truth would prove the tipping point
propelling yet another crash.

Upon the slopes, our sliding hopes:

rare species vanished,
forests leveled,
pages burning,
lesser learning,
glaciers melting,
choices dwindling,
exhausted sources none renew,
vital numbers plunged past zeroes,
worlds crumbling while we look away.

Among my failures, I have found
positions – inches – influence
the constancy of what can stay.

The losses add up.
How they weigh!

Humility has counseled me.

I cannot scapegoat gravity
nor point to physics like a child
who fearfully must pin the guilt
of having busted something dear
on anybody else so he
shall not be grounded, still may play.

Four dump trucks barreled by today,
vibrating windows, glasses, cans.
New billboards boast of new estates.
An architect arrives with plans.

I'll sweep the shards and brace the shelf,
beware of setting any item
nowhere near a pinnacle
nor on the cracked floor with the ants,
just somewhere in the middle way
between the roof, my jar of clay.

It helps me keep things where they are.
Now very little drops too far.

SIGNIFICANT OTHER, SIGNIFYING

A rhetoric of gestures, yes,
when flesh lends definition here:

infinitives within our eyes

    (I find) (your mind)
    (you know) (my soul)

conjunctions wedding sense and breath

linguistic limbs, which intimate
an eloquence no poets grasp.

Semantics whisper kiss to kiss.

Two fluent tongues
translate the flame.

The unheard heartbeats shall proclaim

(as hands can have
their grammar, too)

because such touching needs no verbs.

Our love affirms
above all words..

OUT OF THE LABYRINTH, INTO THE LIGHT

We roamed too far and lost our home,
    directionless, within a daze.

Beyond confusion, voices howled,
    "Escape the madness of your maze!"

We swerved, returned, reversed, and learned
    we're nowhere close to getting out,

so, forward, backward, left, or right,
    we strayed for days, around in doubt.

At some point, we would recognize
    we went this way before, or twice.

We merely had to memorize
    (not wander on like aimless mice)

and map the path - our history -
    to be free of this misery,

then find our exit, at long last.
That's how we came to prize our past.

TO A VENTRILOQUIST

Without as much a twitch of lip,
a captive mouth conveys your voice

> your syllables,
> what you'd project.

You merely whip your wrist around
to simulate the act of speech.

> Your conversations
> none partake.

> Gesticulations
> feigning life:

your halting hand becomes a gawk
or coiled fist mutes everything.

> Direct dictation.
> Pure verbatim.

And, from this, you conclude control.

But then, those thoughts are not their thoughts.
No vocal cords but yours vibrate.

> There's repetition.
> Echoing.

Reverberation of your views.
Some breathing, but no agency.

No spirits lifted, inspiration,
willful praise, participation.

Only cold reiterations.
Tongues compelled to declarations.

    Dead puppets

lifeless microphones
which animate and amplify

    so loudly
    now you fall for it

persuaded in this play of plays
convinced this is *vox populi*

    your people's voice
    agreeably.

I wonder, can you
sense the strings
which set you leaping
with each tug?

How sure are you
no hand commands
the very things
you think you say?

How powerless or free are we?
Let's question all autonomy!

CUBIST DANCERS

Concurrent
silence and the song:

the dancers
motion

all
and none

their ceaseless choreography
as cadenced by eternity

arms opening
to close again

from standing leaps
through spinning
stopped

interpreting infinity
of rhythms
ever fixed

inside the mind

outside of time.

QUANTUM POETICAL

All phrases latent
    until said.

Potential epics
    yet unread.

Entangled notions   speed
    or
    slow
      through pages, spaces.

Verses flow
    from some position
    or one time

    between a rhythm
and a rhyme.

A metaphor of waking light
    emerges from a dreamy night

converging verbs

    divergent choices

    interpretations

    varied voices:

    seas of meaning

        (once obscure)

    now waves
    collapsing
    on the

sure.

RENOVATION OF A SOUL

Gray gossamer of bygone days,
the ash bequeathed by desuetude:

today, the cobwebs must come down
with dust and rusted chandeliers,
the creaking floors and shrieking doors,
the wailing stairs and riddled walls.

Those molded tomes and warping shelves,
the closets of moth-eaten threads,
these peeling ceilings, feeble beams,
the dangling shutters, shorted lamps,
and furnishings no longer fit:
they are to be dislodged for good
along with waste of yesterdays.

The clouded windows shall be cleansed,
tall hedges trimmed, thick vines cut back
so sunlight gilds all halls again
and stagnant shadows may be chased
from any room too like a tomb.

A spotless hearth will blaze anew
and sanctify this space thought cursed.

Let blessings only dwell here, yes,
not one phantasm of the past,
for now begins the exorcism
evicting darkness at long last.

LIMITED OR NO CONNECTIVITY

The networks never let us leave so soon.
Loading, scrolling, streaming – how we scour
to save distractions which our whims devour.
We'll forfeit thought for programs, games, a tune.
From plagues of data, we've grown too immune
to truths, whose questions perish in an hour,
while follows, likes, and squandered social power
transport us backward toward some cool cocoon
where darkness starves potentiality.
We could transcend, be butterflies – reborn!
Instead, most log in, skim and flit, then flee
– no deep connection struck because they're torn
from purpose, promise, and profundity.
They think they live, but this is why we mourn.

TO THE SPIRIT OF MY LION FATHER

Your spirit, it still teaches me
beyond the forests, all I see,
provoking growth and memory
of everything you said to me:

face hunger, risks, the bitter cold
with honor, humbled although bold
when dangers prey, or to survive
– then I must roar with claws and thrive

yet ever be at peace with life,
to never saunter into strife
but guard the pride, my hide and soul,
remaining calmer, in control,

not giving in to instinct's dare
or provocations anywhere
– though not to be completely tame
now I bear forth your noble name.

I journey as one not alone
among the mountains, bones, and stone.
However wind may muss my mane,
I'll shake it off and stake my reign,

a king of self, with strength to lend
the frail who need a loyal friend
who could endure this wild land
with wisdom so to understand

there comes a time for flight or fight
and that the fire's not the light.
Your morals guide me through the night,
revealing might begins with sight,

then steadiness through changing days.
I'll meet the world along my ways
through jungles, deserts, any cave,
and fear no evil. I am brave!

THE TIGRESS TO HER LOVING CUB

Together, on this outcropping,
we mind the wild world in spring

those heavy hooves and hungry howls
the dusty scuffles, savage growls

pursued and prowlers in the reed,
the yawning fawn and tumbleweed

vast stampedes spurred to burst in fear
should crocs or jackals creep too near

the zebras feeding far from harm
as mosquitoes swoop and swarm

nine elephants in sluggish stride
as vultures loop and meerkats hide

serene giraffe, their feast of leaves,
the pregnant mare who huffs and heaves:

how each partakes a primal role,
completes the circle, makes us whole.

Too soon my son you'll join them there
with paws and claws, your awesome stare

while I will watch from near or far
proud of the tiger that you are.

THE WAR WITHIN

Across the rattled battlefield,
between the conflict, cause, and crushed,

another soldier turns to pause
before the dusk of common sense.

This warrior draws in a breath,
contends with death yet does not blink,

but thinks instead – much wondering –
then questions nearly everything.

> *What were the targets of this war?*
> *Which is it I'd be dying for?*
>
> *Why perish here? Why force an end?*
> *What was it that one must defend?*
>
> *Why crash and slash while this world bleeds?*
> *Could peace survive such grievous deeds?*
>
> *Who stands to cede or claim control?*
> *How does the broken become whole?*

And, thus, the deeper struggles start,
beliefs through views, from soul to heart:

to conquer doctrine, self, deceit,
or else live life in full retreat.

ARCHITECTS OF THE IMPOSSIBLE

Come dreamers,
    be our architects!

Escape the grave
    of gravity!

Conceive of castles
    in the clouds

        and break through
        any boundary!

Envision brilliance!
    Stare and dare

        design outside
        the perfect square!

Cast old blueprints
    into the fire

then innovate!
    Surprise! Inspire!

For this is how
we've reached the stars:

not by more horses,
trains, or cars,

but by things that
did not exist.

Refine the science!
    Rise! Persist!

VI.
...through selflessness,
truth's lucid sight...

ESCAPING ESCAPISM

You loathe the known, so roam astray
wherever winds whisk thoughts away.

Forgotten prospects drag the past.
Remembering grounds futures fast.

Which exits lend reprieve from grief
or entrances receive relief?

However we prefer these sprees
through alternate realities,

how many truths could you evade,
ignore, defy, or see delayed?

What situation does one flee?
Escape makes nothing clear or free

when anyplace that speaks release
becomes a space devoid of peace.

If home was mostly feeling right,
we must admit we're wrong tonight.

TELL THEM THE WHOLE TRUTH

Don't prettify our history!

Don't select,

neglect to mention,

or forget

a
single
thing.

When children ask about the world,
what things were like before their birth,
how situations came to be,
or why we choose to live like this,
don't mythicize, romanticize,
or euphemize, or summarize,
or minimize, or sell them lies.

Don't try to bleach the bloody past,
the stains of war, of genocides,
of hatred waged on difference,
the ink of writs injustice penned
with quills dipped into crimson pools
of those who perished needlessly.

Please tell the children EVERYTHING:

the lynchings, riots, old crusades,
the segregations, slaveries,
the slaughtering in names of gods,
the torturing and inquisitions,
the gas chambers, the branded backs,
the Holocaust, internment camps,
the many forms of terrorism,

the colonists, iconoclasts,
deniers of objective facts,
imposters and the hypocrites,
the purchasers of influence,
betrayers of democracy,
exploiters and extremist foes,
the xenophobes, supremacists,
the flaming crosses, nooses, knives,
the drownings, poisons, guillotines,
the napalm, bombs, the casualties,
the crudest cruelest epithets,
the treachery of patriots,
assassinations, obstacles,
the profiling and sexism,
glass ceilings, the intolerance,
the automations of a thought,
the apathy toward suffering,
the plagues and raging ignorance,
defilers and diminishers,
the silencing of dissidence,
the censoring of revelations,
indoctrination, propaganda,
the brainwashers and biased minds,
prejudices everywhere.

And speak of all the better things:

discoveries, inventions, love,
compassion, caring, empathy,
advancements, what was overcome,
of sacrifices, small and large,
the artists, cultures, music, dancing,
the nonconformists, righteous rebels,
revolutions of good cause,
the mastery of elements,
our symbols, myths, antique beliefs,

the architectures of the ages,
agriculture, gatherers,
sciences and scholarship,
enlightenment, imagination,
the poetries of everyone,
the curing and the nurturing,
the fallen tyrants, toppled walls,
the peace once gained, to be regained,
defenders of our liberty,
the freedom that is never free,
our never-ending fights for rights,
the whistleblowers and disclosures,
the challenges we rise to meet,
adventures waged against all odds,
society and synergy,
togetherness, equality,
the strength of individuals,
the champion someone could be,
the beauty of diversity,
the questions of profundity,
integrity, the bond of trust,
our bravery to face unknowns
and hopefulness for what must come.

Do tell the children everything.

Let honesty relieve us from
repeating tragic past mistakes.

Let history inform our need
to teach the children everything

because you know
they would find out

eventually

then wonder why

ROBERT J TIESS

you'd look them in the eye
and lie.

THE HIDDEN OPTIMISTS

Somewhere in this dismal district,
obscured behind the queasy thrum
of engines ever trembling,
and sweatshops overrun by greed,
and mutterings of much despair,
and angers brewing everywhere,

a kindness thrives,
a bright mind grows

unlikely love becomes and knows
a blessedness awaits outside
these squalid streetscapes made to hide
the promise of a better day.

In spite of that,
please hear them pray:

the voice no noises drown or still,
the faithful ones by windowsills,
those poets who extol the light,
the wakeful dreamers keeping night
from darker horror, smog, or hate.

No concrete here constrains their fate.

VALUATION

In one of my utopias,
you could enjoy a cup of tea
for jotting haiku on a napkin.
A limerick wins you lunch or dinner.

Odes may pay for groceries.
Two quatrains get you on the train.
A sonnet cycle buys the car.
An epic puts you in a house!

I've yet to spell the details out
--the ballad or the terza rima,
what they'd purchase in this place,
and then the whole economy.

The shares, the bonds, the interest rates.
How word banks would lend eloquence.
Reserves of verse worth more than gold.
My fictive little fantasy.

Yet how much richer life might be
if we'd invest less in expense
and more in our phraseology.
Such dividends. Such profiting!

No precious gems or metals fill
my thoughts with fortunes high and bright.
Just quote me Frost or Angelou,
and I'd be wealthy through the night!

RIGHTS OF PASSAGE

As openly whole oceans flow
and willingly the winds will blow

let life deliver, give, and drift
around a mountain, through the rift

beneath, beside, before, behind,
above the hurdles of the mind

between the silence of two words,
and soar across your thoughts like birds

whose wings embrace the gift of flight
and, with it, distance, height, and sight

to seek the freedom, find a way
beyond denial or delay

where everything commences so
as openly whole oceans flow.

PERSONAL COPERNICAN REVOLUTION

When your world
               (moved)
   grows humble

small

   essential
   (yes)

          yet less
          than
          all

   – no center
   to the cosmic roll –

but one

   (of countless
   none control)

in orbit outside
     pride's high view:

         the universe
         is not just you.

NECESSARY SEPARATION

Between the streams of patterned drops,
    the world remained just as it was

    beneath the beams of breaking light
    met weeks ago in brighter times

– the difference being,
on this night,

she could observe the storms defined
apart from what once seemed to be:

    that necessary separation

        detaching vision
        from emotion,

        a dawn of objectivity

        when weather
        and perceptions fade

    and suddenly
    the mind might see
    such rain suggests no sadness, pain,
    nor anything so sad or vain;

it's just a mixture of conditions,

atmospherics,
transient,
precipitation of the hour.

At last,
she knew
she had that power.

THE SONG OF WALT IS OUR SONG

Walt Whitman,
bless our multitudes:

we congregate

we consecrate

we celebrate and sing ourselves
among your loves
for life

our lives.

We excavate your heart of truth.

We venerate and venture forward
arm in arm

embrace ourselves

as you, with you, together, now.

We meditate on what we were.

We speculate on who we'd be.

We cultivate our lives with light
beginning with this mirroring

reflecting in each other's eyes

to see how much we are alike

to know the warmth that only comes
when we stand closer
side by side.

Unwritten maps upon our palms,

we navigate at night
by touch

the intimacies brushed by love
when we step past our broken bones
and hold devotion
soul to soul.

We advocate

we adulate

commemorate you, liberator,

who dreamt past time-worn mortal coils
exceeding meager meter's edges,
boundlessly shrugged measured plans
for measureless exuberance

you renegade of cadenced thought

veering

gearing

hymnals spinning

rhythms lending such sedition
candid hearts must dance with chance

like lithe subversive ballerinas loathing hints of inhibition
twirling, prancing
mischievous, precarious
thrusts uncontrived by comely choice

(yet inwardly ascension-bent
so impulse wholly conquers limits,
slips from chains of disciplines)

thus bursting forthright
night by sighing dream
by trying day

by artless fits

impassioning

if crashing
craft

vivacious arts
unbridled starts

dismissing limbs from stillness, death
for fevered whims
or sovereign leaps

while drumming from torrential songs
storm fiery in primal heartbeats pounding hotter by the hour

percussive wondrous

feet-first thunders
crushing unabashed ballet
conveying restless zestful feelings

words reeling toward their rightful arias
however long, beloved, wrong.

Go gallivant, enchant, descant as skylarks soaring
– hark, they sing!

Their fragile strainings fortify our infinitely cosmic song
heard over forests yawning older than language, crying, history

(not nearly drowned out by the rivers rushing
flooding muddied fields

sunken plains where all may gaze
but none must tread

if we are getting
anywhere)

past chapels full of searchers, sinners,

forgivers joining non-believers,
grievers of ephemera,
old gilded crosses, echoed prayers,
cracked wedding bells divorced from time

downward
deeper

down
to
earth

outpacing every trail we lost
eternally
externally

if evidenced to be so found
if imprecisely

just right
there

to follow, leave,
conceive, receive

regardless how impetuous
a muse might choose to be at last:

let unheard verses voice the way
with beauty's incandescent truth
from freedom's blazing lips to say
the lyrics of our wondrous song.

Bright music calls us to belong!

PAS DE DEUX

A dancer glances past her song,
    steps back in time
        to there:
            he whirls
    to catch her
    once she leaps too long

    then slips.

Red rhythms twist
as tendons burn.

-- the duet moves outside routine

    apart from when,
  beyond return,

to orchestrate one need unseen

    till now
    as music leaves the hall

    and one heart's leap
prevents a fall.

TRANSCENDING DIALECTICS

Go, seekers!
> Leave those old extremes!

> Surpass that frontier
> of what seems.

Exhaust perception, what was sought.

> From nuanced truths
> > gain sharper thought

> than anything
> sensed yesterday.

Embrace the gray,
the middle way.

With temperance
> and empathy
> receive
> your new reality.

INSIDE COLLAPSING MINES OF HOPE

Some tunnelers turn rescuers,
retracing walls and bracing paths

through sinking fear and blinding dust
with urgency past broken trust.

They prop up rock, the failing beam
that lets a passage see collapse,

though others slump defeatedly,
give into chills, a fearful lapse,

then let their shadows block the way
between their lives and light of day

when everyone should strike at stone,
risk injury, a broken bone,

expending all essential breath
to fend against the threat of death.

As torches fade, and all goes dark,
it may well come to that one spark

of perseverance in a voice
or optimism in a choice:

the thing that lends a golden glow
wherever wonder dims to woe

just long enough to kindle hope
so some proceed while others cope

until the excavation's done
and all resurface in the sun.

VII.

*...where peace and love
lead life from night...*

WITHSTANDING

Amid the rubble, marble hands,
ten fingers firmly interlocked,
the arms broke off from figures crushed
in struggles of another age.

Not much remains, but this is all
one needs to see when wondering
if love could bear the savage wrath
of weather, war, and centuries.

No magnitude of havoc has
undone that clutch, that fierce embrace
of soul mates I can almost see,
their gaze cemented, eyes to eyes,

no words about to part their kiss
because their touch is voice enough
to vouch how love withstands a fall
and nothing shall erase it all.

UNFINISHED SYMPHONY

My ways, uncharted melodies,
because they will be improvised.

My rhythms drift, resisting time,
for every tempo must be mine.

These dreams, unfinished symphonies.
My violins ascend to sing.

I am conductor, player, sound,
the maestro of myself, I found.

SACRED FLIGHT

What endless steps and ramps were raised
by those who hoped to cross the gates
between this globe
and paradise.

Then
escalators, elevators
charging upward through the sky

propellers, jets, and rocketry
all following to fly.

Some strained for stars,
held moon in hands.

Most never found their promised lands

so technical yet unawares
that scaling heaven's hidden stairs
was not a worldly quest

ascension only possible
when mortal thoughts divest
all trappings of their earthly ways
and journey as a soul.

To find this way, you lose the world.
Relinquish false control.

Become one with the universe,
the weightless peace of light

transcending everything once known
to scale the sacred flight.

TAO

Within this flowing,
        I shall know
        the ways of nature
        where I'll go

attuned to life,
        the path ahead,
        where past and present
        love then wed

and birth the future
        where we meet
        without delay,
        without deceit,

in harmony
        with stars and dust
        once we begin
        to see and trust

the universe
        unfolds and thrives
        just like the lotus
        of our lives.

LOVE'S SPECIAL RELATIVITY

A union of coordinates
from where we stand
and who we were
to how we reach
eternal love:

our special relativity

encircling
endless energy

inertial births
new-sprung from mass

no sooner flowing
knowing
showing

referential

fixed
yet going

embodying velocities
in fields of possibilities

framing moments
lost to sight

found
how bound

now boundless
by our constant light.

VALEDICTION

Schoolmaster clears his weary throat,
prepares to wake the restless class
adorned in black robes, mortarboards,
gold tassels swaying in the wind
as raspy words rag at their ears
which listen more to rising tides.

His written speech reads faintly here
beneath the sunlight burning bold.
The podium, though formidable,
accentuates his failing frame.
The microphone, that spiteful thing,
exaggerates each wheeze and gasp.

His words intend to send souls forth,
provoke fresh spirits, impel hearts,
invoke old wisdom, thrill, inspire,
to lend new masters ancient fire
--Promethean, as he would say--
but something slips away today.

What were the points of looking backward,
resurrecting Orpheus,
referring to Bellerophon,
exhuming myths from tomes and tombs,
upsetting dust from bloodless times?
These young ones mustn't give a damn.

Above the field seagulls sing
and circle the suspension bridge
that arches over charging waves
where many minds here swim or sail.
No eloquence can call them back

to this commencement exercise.

Reviving lost Odysseus,
he warns of getting swept to sea,
reversing fortunes, metaphors
to muster up profundity
as caps get cast into the air
as if he is no longer there,

at most a roaming ghostly moan
to haunt some unread denizen,
an eager Socrates few heed
when all learn fast to graduate,
become the novel, next the past,
and then the questions rarely asked.

BUILDING THE ARK OF LOVE

Confusion floods then drowns the hours,
and anything we held was ours
splits and drifts off in the surge
of dread and doubt's most fervent urge
to perish in uncertainty.

An ocean of perplexity
swells and crashes reason's beach,
surpasses sandbags, soon will reach
these hills where lasting hopes retreat
and disbelief brings self-defeat

as answers sink behind the tide.
But now, with nowhere left to hide,
let's band together here, and fast,
preserve the future through the past,
recalling faith, how to survive,

believe we can and must revive
the beauty, justice, trust, and peace
that only thrives once we release
our eyes from color, hearts from hate,
all cause from warfare, choice from fate.

Why brood, presuming tragedy,
when we could use our unity
– our grace and ingenuity –
to craft an ark of love to save
our good world from an early grave?

Enlisting every empathy,
be conquered by love's need for peace.
Surrender. Gather. Plan to build.

ROBERT J TIESS

We have the hammers, wood, and nails!
Assemble, friends, so truth prevails!

LODESTARS

Entwined inside this midnight tapestry,
rich threads of finespun interstellar light
edged with planets, moons, and nebulae:
your constellation dawns to set me right

so I may pilot outside yellowed charts
of olde worlds we would coolly navigate
to plot new routes through strange and unknown parts
where others fled or dread to speculate.

You schooled me how to hoist these royal sails,
deflect from tempests, read these unclear skies,
respect the oceans, every wave, the whales,
and never capsize in my heavy sighs.

A savvy captain, steering clear with might,
I maintain faith throughout the doubtful night
and seize again upon your sage advice:
avoid all sirens, pirates, ice,

observe auroras, sea birds, any sign
of prospect, risk, deceit, or mutiny
confusing neither gold, desires, wine
as honest compasses toward destiny.

I sometimes glimpse you beaming past the moon
inclined and kind to mind me motherly
intent that nothing, nowhere, should maroon
your only son within this ruthless sea.

With every new adventure you remain
the wind inspiriting every enterprise.
When all is lost, I scope those steady stars
in hopes to spy your proud and guiding eyes.

THE ART OF ROCK BALANCING

Unevenness invariably
    resists the balance wanted here,
        which means
    you always must do more
than set
    a stone
        on top of stone.
        Determine centers patiently.
Collaborate with gravity,
    the shape
        and weight
        of each thing placed,
proceeding with
    such gentleness
        that nothing
    topples
        from
        your
    touch.

DREAMING BEYOND STAIRWAYS

Our
steps
adjacent
upping down

      then
      exits
      entered
   bend around

as if
reflecting
Escher prints
I saw before
you fell asleep.

      Here nowhere
      shows expectedly

     or losing ground
   is what we
keep

unless
   one means
      to rove around.

Yes
  I can ask
     what logic found
        if it descends
           an endless
              flight

          yet
    wound up
    doubting right
    from rite

(or is it leave
you've left
behind?)

At
times
a landing
clears my mind

to glimpse above
a floor or
fall

and know
(behind your door)
no wall
keeps *ever afters*
from this dream

where higher inclines often seem
to draw me toward
    that wish to be
    the destination where
    you're free
        to
        cross
    the threshold of old eyes
without
a need
to grieve

goodbyes.

ALL IN THEIR TIMES

All in their times

fresh meadows bloom

a robin grabs at grass for nests

a weathered fence withstands no wind

old bones revive dead histories

one bridge unites divided lands

a bolt of lightning sparks a forest

waterfalls slow into ice

storm clouds recede beyond the sky

sailboats traverse the widest seas

four bouquets pass through graveyard gates

ten textbooks burn

young teachers learn

as graduates receive degrees

three wheels squeal their last full turn

two cubs shrug off their winter sleep

five eagles climb

six seagulls dive

eight rocks grow smoother in the waves

a seventh lotus flows from mud

a desert starved of rain gains floods

the canyon lets an echo go

eleventh hours pass by night

the violin will play its part

nine butterflies arise in flight

as infants glimpse beginning's light.

DEEPMOST

How deeply runs
    this course
    of love?

    Oceanic.

Fathomless.

And
    diveable
        if you
        could hold
            your
            breath
            until
            the
            end
            of
            time.

EMBLAZON

Your eyes light my horizon, love:
    my days arise within your sight,
    and, when you gaze away, that's night.

How you've become my alphabet,
    a part of every word I breathe,
    essential to my meaning now.

You're like the bible of my faith,
    the genesis of testaments,
    the truth of revelations.

You press on my piano heart
    releasing music from my soul:
    those melodies but we compose.

Inside your mind, beyond all math,
    I find the one, the sum of us,
    equation past infinity.

Our galleries of memories
    make moments into works of art:
    a beauty framed in timelessness.

In truth, you move my universe,
    bring starlight to my wandering world,
    where life begins to rise again.

SOUL WINDOWS

    We scoured ceilings, walls, and floors
in search of spaces, breaks, or doors,

    so we'd be free of what divides
obscures, forbids, deceives, or hides.

    A slit of sun delivered skies,
disclosing what escaped our eyes:

    the wider world we've never seen,
the measureless, and what's between.

    A simple window was our goal,
enough light to revive a soul

    and show us where some truth had passed
or answers lived for questions asked.

    Such revelations beckoned there,
beyond our earth, that sea, the air!

    It humbles us to come so far
then start to wonder where we are.

SEMESTER'S END AT RAPHAEL'S SCHOOL OF ATHENS

A spirit drifts down corridors
once humming with philosophy

    (curricula in limbo's grip)

   now silence lectures everything

  between thick pillars
  fi ne ly cra ck ed,
  old studies
  rid of inquiry,

  foundations of indifference:

  this campus of our ignorance.

Hence, spectral lessons test your schooling,
    graduates, who thought it done:

  your dialogues, debating, doubt.

A phantom of awareness pleads,
    Have you surveyed your knowledge yet?

    Will you be humbled or forget
    oblivion consumes us all?

Old ghosts of truth haunt every hall.

They wait to see who shrinks or drinks,
who flees, decrees, deceives, or leaves
the cavern of the prideful lie,
    then steps toward light,
      by asking
        why.

AFTERPOEM

TOWARD WISDOM FROM HUMILITY

Past vanity,
        I climb to see
                beyond the country
                      of myself:

a frontier rich
        with revelations,
                interpretations,
                      further views,

then questions,
        endless wonderment,
                through selflessness,
                      truth's lucid sight,

where peace
        and love
                lead life
                      from night.

= ADDENDA =

ABOUT ME

I am a poet in New York State, where I've lived all my life. I've been writing poetry since I was a child in the 1980s. I earned my degree in English Literature at SUNY New Paltz, and I have been enjoying a wonderful professional career of public service at my local library since the 1990s.

As a lifelong advocate of public libraries, I must interrupt myself to say this:

> If you haven't visited your local library in a while, or ever, please do. Public libraries provide educational and enrichment opportunities for their communities. Many of them offer story time for children, book discussions for adults, public events and concerts for all ages, research services, art exhibits, author and genre-based reading recommendations, special collections such as local history and genealogical documents, access to local and other government information, current and past newspapers, scholarly journals, general and specialized encyclopedias, article databases, free online courses and language learning, along with electronic books and digital streaming services for movies, audiobooks, and music.

If you haven't already, please consider contacting your nearest library to inquire about the possibility of getting a library card. Thank you for your patience. (I love libraries!) Back on topic now.

Journey is the word I think of most when I try to describe my life, especially my writing life. My journey as writer goes back to my childhood, when my mother, Jeannette, established my very first library at home. She gradually filled up shelves with volumes of all sorts that would nurture my love of reading, learning, and writing. There were dictionaries, vocabulary workbooks, poetry and short story anthologies, books on art, math, space, history, zoology, dinosaurs, mythology, and more.

Those two bookcases seemed to hold the cosmos of information. It was such fun leaping book to book, and that activity would prepare me to travel more interdisciplinary paths through subjects such as art, music, literary studies, psychology, mathematics, computer science, and philosophy. This was pre-World Wide Web, but I can see it was all rather hypertextual, with me vaulting between volumes and shelves instead of websites.

What a joy it was – and still is – to happen upon a new topic and gradually learn there was even more to it than I anticipated. That incremental awareness would lead me to expect there was almost always more to anything I observed. It's like standing at the bottom of what you might have thought was a small, ordinary hill, and then the sun comes out, the fog clears, and you realize the hill keeps going – that it's actually a mountain, one of several ahead – and the way forward becomes the way up.

It can be a humbling but triumphant kind of graduation as you ascend that mountain of learning. Feelings of intimidation, insignificance, fatigue, or defeat can deplete any sense of progress and send you tumbling back down the mountain, much in the manner of the mythical figure Sisyphus, who was condemned to roll his boulder up a slope repeatedly, to no avail. Each time he neared the top, the rock slipped from his fingers and rolled away.

When I began publishing, there was no boulder in sight. I saw some success with my earliest submissions being accepted for publication, and I felt like I was on my way, but the apparent hill I thought I passed proved to be more mountainous than I allowed at that young age, when achievements felt like the natural, if not expected results of a good effort. The fog of youth had not cleared yet, and I had yet to discover what the real journey ahead would entail.

From certain angles, the mountain may seem approachable, easy enough, but, as grass fades into rock, elevation gains, angles sharpen, and the terrain turns unpredictable or more hazardous. Each step demands increased attention and resilience, especially when you find yourself before your first major impasse or precipice.

The more I looked around while trying to climb my figurative mountain as a writer, the more it became painfully obvious that there was a vast valley between what I had written and where I really wanted to be as a writer. To get there, I would have to learn more, do more, relinquish old thoughts and habits, and venture beyond the small country of myself.

That's how I came to voluntarily pause my poetry submissions in the late 1990s. I dearly needed to focus on my craft, develop my ideas, breathe in life, absorb new information, witness more perspectives, deepen my empathy, and wonder much. During that interlude, I began my career in the library world, and, at home, I immersed myself more deeply in my art and music and worked on a variety of literary projects, such as expanding upon my quasi-quantum literary metatheory, *Interpreture*.

I wrote poems in that time but gave almost no thought to publishing them, although my mother, who was perhaps my biggest fan and most honest critic, encouraged me to review, revise, and publish my work. I promised I would publish something, someday, once I felt I could write something that might be worthy of being read. It wasn't a question of self-esteem. I needed to improve. Years later, in publishing this collection of my newest poems, I'm finally getting to deliver on that promise. I only wish she could have read this book before she passed away in 2020.

I wish my father could have read this, too. He passed away before I attended college. In his lifetime, he knew I loved to write, draw, and create things, and he encouraged that in his own ways. He bought me my first computer, which was an incredible gift.

I quickly got into word processing and taught myself BASIC (a computer programming language). Months later, I was fortunate to have some ideas and programs of mine published in computer magazines while he was still alive.

As a professional teacher, and as an avid amateur radio operator at home, my father loved to communicate with people near and far. Sometimes he spoke only in code – morse code, that is. Through the gentle but steady flickering of a telegraph key, he instantly encoded words into controlled bursts of short and long beeps ("dots" or "dits" and "dashes" or "dahs"), which were briskly decoded and replied to by other "hams" (operators), who could be streets, towns, states, or countries away.

His radios glowed with dials, meters, and frequency numbers, while his oscilloscopes transformed voices into deliriously dancing lines on screens. I remember how he'd lean toward a microphone and repeat the letters "C Q" in an effort to reach other operators – and then how he would spell out his official alphanumeric "call sign" using a standardized "phonetic alphabet": "Whisky Bravo Two Foxtrot November Papa" (WB2FNP). And then there were times he'd wade into rivers of static, flipping switches and adjusting dials in hopes of hearing another voice through the noise.

All of this was spectacular to hear and behold. Knowing how inquisitive I could get, he would sometimes turn to me in his wooden swivel chair, and patiently explain how certain things worked, from the technology that converted speech into radio transmissions to how those signals were broadcast and transformed back into sound by distant receivers. It was amazing to learn that, as invisible to us they are, radio waves occur further along the same "electromagnetic spectrum" that also gives us visible light – the very light we see – and that there was such a thing as "radio astronomy" which used "radio telescopes" to reveal things in the universe that would remain otherwise invisible to regular (optical) telescopes. I often wonder what else I could have learned from him had he not died so young of cancer.

Between the informational instincts and creative encouragements of my mother and my father's aptitude for education and communication, I have become increasingly aware of how their approaches to life influenced my existence as well as my creative inclinations once I entered adulthood. The more I see beyond myself, the more I realize I should be grateful to everyone – and I do mean everyone – who contributed to my life in every conceivable way, directly or indirectly, including all those innumerable and unknown persons who, every day, help to sustain the world and to make this existence what it is.

A lifetime wouldn't be enough to thank them all – the farmers and food preparers, builders and beautifiers, healers and helpers, drivers and discoverers, creators and critics, conductors and nonconformists, authors, artists, scientists, dreamers, advocates and activists, futurists and historians, traditionalists and trailblazers, skeptics and believers, seekers and scholars, provokers and peace-makers – and everyone else. I am grateful for you all.

I also very deeply appreciate the responses I have received from various readers and poets around the world since I resumed publicizing my poetry as of a few years ago. I became a frequent competitor at AllPoetry.com, participating in over 1,500 poetry contests and writing prompts. Opening myself up to public commentary and criticism, in real time, was somewhat unnerving yet exhilarating. I'm glad I did it, as that helped me believe a little bit more in the writing and ideas I wanted to share with the world.

In December 2021, I joined Twitter, and some of my poetry posts eventually gained responses and appreciation from readers, poets, and others. I appreciate that kindness and interest in my work, but I am also aware that I cannot become complacent as a writer. I must keep working on my writing in order to earn the honor of connecting with more readers.

One way I hope to do that is to try to remain a mostly accessible writer while staying true to what I want to express. While that might sound easy, it isn't. I've studied poetics, literary theory, criticism, etc., but, all that bookish stuff aside, my real wish is to craft and share more relatable poetic experiences with people from all walks of life. I want to welcome everyone into my poetry so they can feel at ease, at home, and, in some sense, appreciated and respected, possibly even represented, at various points, in my works.

Since I do not write for any one particular audience or persuasion, I feel free to celebrate diversity while striving for inclusivity throughout my poetry. I write on an expanding range of topics through different viewpoints and writing styles. There are some things I do try to be consistent with, such as composing my poems to be read aloud. I try to invest attention in the acoustics and musicality of a poem. The assonance, consonance, alliteration, rhyming, crescendos, and legato or staccato passages you might hear in my poems – all of that is usually intentional.

I tend to think about a lot of things when I write and revise. One day I decided to jot down a bunch of topics that came to mind when I would review my work. I roughly grouped those subjects under headings, which I further simplified. The product of that exercise is something I light-heartedly nicknamed *My Eleven M's of Poetry*:

> meaning, movement, metaphor, musicality, manifestations, mystery, measurement, mechanics, momentum, mythology, and memorability.

I include this amusing little list here as a very small window into some of my thoughts when I evaluate my work, and I elaborate on these *M's* a bit more in the next section.

When I write, sometimes I think of outer space. Just as the metaphysical poet John Donne recognized "No man is an island... Every man is a piece of the continent," I recognize no poem or literary form of expression exists alone, apart, or within a perfect vacuum: each work has its presence – dimension, mass, and physics – within the literary cosmos, which expands in all directions and glows with countless stellar writers encircled by worlds of their own.

Among the many luminaries I admire are Maya Angelou, Billy Collins, Mary Oliver, Robert Frost, Emily Dickinson, Walt Whitman, E.E. Cummings, Elizabeth Barret Browning, Ted Kooser, Langston Hughes, T.S. Eliot, John Keats, and others I'll mention and recommend later in this book. On any night, I can imagine looking up and marveling at entire constellations of their poetic brilliance while I drift somewhere between what I never said, what I failed to phrase, all the better words escaping me at any moment, and what I believe I might still express if I could only make more progress as a poet and a person. The education yet to come is truly *endless* (like humility, as Eliot once noted).

There's so much to be learned and unlearned. This universe of literature provokes us to be students, voyagers, and discoverers: it continuously evolves as its potentials turn kinetic, and it expands to encompass every conceivable expression since the very first word was enunciated at the dawn of human history. Even as I write this, creative energy surges elsewhere throughout that expanse, transforming moments into memories and inspiration, imagination into ideas and insights, and then words into meaning and influences with their own singular properties, mass, gravity, trajectories, and momentum.

At any point, at any moment, the slightest light or transformative intensity of anyone's words or ideas can flow in any direction – past to future, future to present, present to eternity, or toward timelessness or distant worlds of thought either visible, unseen, or yet to take their final shapes around newly ignited stars emerging as points of inspiration on any given day. Every single last thing – imagined or expressed – in this dreamy, immeasurable space, however seemingly insignificant, will always be an essential part of the whole – of the synergy of expression – and will register, relate, absorb or relay energy, and really matter, for now and always, all the way down to the ever-fluctuating quantum scape of infinite and indeterminate possibilities still to be observed and understood.

What a humbling yet heartening prospect that is to me.

MY "ELEVEN M'S OF POETRY"

A lot of thoughts, memories, and questions stream through my mind when I write. When I reach a point where I want to review and revise a poem, there are certain areas I tend to focus on – apparently *eleven* of them!

I have jokingly called this makeshift checklist my *Eleven M's of Poetry*. I'm sharing these definitions here, in no particular order, simply to provide small windows into some of my thoughts when I write and revise:

Meaning: What a poem means, intentionally or potentially. Also, how meanings might arise from abstract or concrete ideas or images, and how those things could promote potential interpretations.

Movement: How a poem flows (verbally, structurally), or how it can move (affect, inspire) a reader (e.g. emotionally). Sometimes it means where a poem begins, goes, and then ends – how much distance it covers, how it navigates that journey, and where it arrives, if anywhere.

Metaphor: The nature and effectiveness of a poem's metaphor(s) or metaphoric thinking (in which I would include similes). Is the metaphor consistent? Could it be extended? Have I mixed metaphors?

Musicality: The meters/rhythms and audible/musical aspects of a poem, including its smooth (legato) or choppy (staccato) phrasing, pauses (caesurae), rhyming, harmony (euphony) or harshness (cacophony), or repetitions of word sounds (alliteration, assonance, consonance).

Manifestations: What a poem represents or reveals. More generally (as I use the term here) how a poem can communicate its representations and revelations through words, ideas, imagery, intimations, etc. Also, what a reader sees "manifesting" (directly or indirectly) in (or from) each poem.

Mystery: What questions a poem might pose, approach, attempt to answer, or leave unresolved. I sometimes think of this in the context of what the Romantic poet John Keats once described (in a letter to his brothers) as "negative capability," the ability to remain in an unresolved state of uncertainty. Some poems can mystify or perplex, while others could be more forthcoming and revelatory.

Measurement: The physical or conceptual dimensions of a poem, especially how words, ideas, images, lines, stanzas, sections, style(s), etc. "scale" within a poem's overall construction (i.e. the poem's arrangement of ideas, words, lines, stanzas) as well as its theoretical capacity (e.g. a small poem with "big questions" or a long poem on a simple or more intimate theme).

Mechanics: The internal workings/physics of the poem as well as the engineering and synergy of all the poem's individual elements. If a poem seems "mechanical" in some way, was that the intended effect?

Momentum: How quickly ideas are (or should be) developed in the course of the poem its overall velocity of phrasing, lineation, thoughts, rhyming, imagery, etc.

Mythology: The mythical or mythopoeic aspects of the poem. This consideration can include archetypes, symbols, connections or allusions to other myths/ literary works, and more.

Memorability: How memorable a poem might be after it has been read. Also, which words, images, or ideas might stand out or become memorable to a reader? This is probably the most difficult and subjective consideration in this list.

These oversimplifications, of course, and incomplete. My considerations and approaches will vary with each poem and include things not listed above.

More than anything else, I try to let a poem decide where it wants to go, how it wants to get there, what it wants to say, and so forth. That's why my poems often take on different voices, tones, shapes, and sizes. Some verses alight on topics, linger momentarily, and then flit away like blissful butterflies. Or a poem might put on a tux and speak formally, while another might wear a nightgown and whisper with an amorous air of mystery, all while yet another poem dances uninhibited around a page by moonlight. And then there can be those poems that will walk up hills or climb trees or mountains just to catch a sunrise, or to observe a bird, or to simply stare up at the heavens in hopes of spotting a shooting star.

As I accompany my poems into familiar or unknown territories, I am like a constant traveler, ever anticipating another destination, sometimes an adventure, or a moment of pure awe. Along the way, I'm grateful to reach a calm resting place, a fresh vista, or some unexpected discovery. At some point, I must part with one poem and venture onward with another, but, as my journey brings me around again, I return to earlier poems to see if they're happy where they are, or if they'd rather go elsewhere.

Sometimes I don't have to ask. I can hear it in their voices or see it in their eyes, and I'll just wait there beside them until they have an inkling of what they want say or do next. Some just want to chat for a while, or think out loud, or sing at random, or scream into the wind. Not long ago, a haiku poem of mine started to think it wanted to be a sonnet instead. Then it wanted to be something else. It wasn't really sure, and I knew not to force it. A few days later, it was happy to live on as haiku.

Each expression must find its own path into the world, just like each of us. I prefer to see my poems reach some sense of completeness, to know the joy of life is not absent even when they are sad, scared, or serious. I hope my poems get to travel and eventually can make friends with readers. I try to be supportive and understanding, even when they're not in a mood to talk much to anyone. I must stay patient, listen, and love them all. That's the least I can do for my poems, as their father.

=== THREE BRIEF ESSAYS ===

ESSAY I: HUMILITY & SOCRATES

Socrates, an ancient Greek philosopher, gained fame and a swift death sentence for challenging the ideas and authorities of his day. He turned discussions into debates, asked provocative questions, continuously raised contentious observations, and disputed misconceptions, assumptions, and untruths as he encountered them.

Now, that doesn't sound very humble, does it? There's more, though.

Though the writings of Plato and Xenophon (two other philosophers who were students of Socrates) we learn Socrates began his legendary deliberations in an inquisitive tone, situating himself as someone seeking to comprehend something more completely and truthfully. This effective tactic lured other debaters to say things Socrates could then deconstruct, scrutinize, and refute.

Where's the humility in that? We'll soon see.

Even though Socrates railed against dubious assertions, time and again, he also understood, in a very public way, the nature of knowledge and how careful anyone must be in claiming *I know*. Even as he exasperated peers and was considered by many to be corruptive, dangerous, and repulsive, Socrates recognized he was not perfect.

In fact, Socrates openly proclaimed his own *lack of knowledge* – fully admitting to his ignorance without hesitation or pride – and that's why the Oracle of Delphi would consider Socrates the "wisest" person in Athens at that time.

In "The Humbling," the title poem of this collection, the narrator refers to this paradoxical nature of Socrates – the humility of the learner who must concede self-knowledge of ignorance:

> I'm just a student, one who sees
> the paradox of Socrates,
>
> to understand I do not know
> and yet enlighten as I go

I sometimes see Socrates as either a personification of philosophy itself or, more generally, as a fitting representative of philosophy's many questioners. As there is much wondering and a quest for understanding throughout this poetry collection, I chose my digital artwork, *Socrates: Lessons for the Nescient, or Semester's End in Raphael's School of Athens*, for this book's cover image.

The setting of my image visually alludes to *School of Athens* by Raphael, a Renaissance painter. In 1511, he finished painting that lively masterpiece, populating it with Plato, Socrates, Aristotle, and many other thinkers engaged in various discussions and metaphysical musings. The swarming image seems to capture philosophy's etymological "love of wisdom" while framing it, most appropriately, I would say, within a classical architecture illuminated by the warm artistic radiance of the Renaissance.

My own visual interpretation of the school occurs at a later time than in Raphael's work. In my image, the trial of Socrates has concluded. Socrates the man is gone from the world. Evening has arrived, and the Renaissance sheen has dimmed considerably as the ghostly figure of Socrates floats hauntingly through halls once teeming with some of the biggest questions ever posed. Philosophy has lost one of its most devoted champions, but queries linger, will not die.

Behind my apparitional Socrates, ruins obscure the tempestuous horizon. To his left, rising wind and mottled light filters through tattered drapes. To his right, miniature nested dome ceilings remain suspended in the air, unsupported in a surreal manner. Foreground items include a vessel and chalice, a shackle undone, and a blank scroll unfurled and cascading over the stairs. Chipped remnants of ornamental patterns surrounding the scene no longer bear the burnished sheen of Raphael's majestic setting.

I'll leave it to the reader to consider the interpretive potential of these symbolic elements within the contexts of philosophy, Socrates' life and tragic end, and our own daily searches for truth. It may help us to know Socrates so prized what he considered the well-examined life that, when it became evident people did *not* share in his inviolable fact-finding mission, he accepted sacrifice long before renouncing his cause of truth. Then he ingested the hemlock poison prescribed as punishment for his philosophical practices.

From certain angles, Socrates, imperfect as he was, can be seen simultaneously as a humbled and a humbling figure. He has died, but he has not faded, nor can he be made to disappear entirely from our lives. With a bit of poetic license, I can imagine the spirit of Socrates imploring anyone who would hear him to keep raising essential questions, especially in matters of knowledge and authority. Sadly, our present reality makes this a difficult request to anyone across the world: neither free speech nor intellectual freedom exists universally for all, and any attempts to be a champion of objective truth can be dangerous or deadly, depending on where someone lives.

Elsewhere in the world, state-controlled media prevents reliable information from flowing everywhere, while its own propaganda and deceptions continue to spread far and fast. The speed, insecurity, and exploitation of our current information technology further complicates these grave matters. The most advanced artificial intelligence has not relieved our daily need for debates and human fact-checkers around the clock. We will always need a kind of Socrates, it seems: someone who would value truth over self and everything else.

Benjamin Franklin, inventor, writer, and one of America's most famous "Founding Fathers," penned something in his *Autobiography* that I think is useful to mention at this point. In his ninth chapter ("Plan for Attaining Moral Perfection"), Franklin drew up a list of thirteen virtues. Like Socrates (and nearly all other mortals), Franklin fell short of perfecting his morality (e.g. being a latecomer to the cause of abolition). Still, Franklin did recognize the importance of humility and cited it as the crowning virtue of his plan. Beneath "Humility," Franklin advised, "Imitate Socrates and Jesus."

Anyone familiar with the lives of Socrates and Jesus Christ can attest to how difficult their examples would be to imitate. I sometimes wonder if that might have been one of Franklin's more subtle points, consciously or subconsciously, most of all with Jesus: such moral perfection – if it is seriously suggested as being attainable by anyone less than God – would require the rarest of extraordinary human beings of the highest integrity and compassion, the purest lifestyle and faith, the strongest stamina and wisdom, the greatest selflessness and humility, not to mention a complete willingness to face public crucifixion and total sacrifice for truth and for the sins of others.

Any suggestion of emulation would be problematic: it invites us toward potential missteps and misunderstanding as we attempt to be more like other persons, especially when doing that without the essential awareness and experiences defining those persons' minds and lives. Also, our motivations and reasoning would not be identical to theirs, leading to all sorts of possible misjudgments throughout these well-intended but fatally flawed endeavors.

Thankfully, we can garner guidance and inspiration from people without having to abandon ourselves entirely. In addition to Socrates and Jesus, there we might find and learn from other humble individuals in our lives, be they friends or relatives or historic and well-known public figures like Mother Teresa, Mahatma Gandhi, Jane Goodall, Thich Nhat Hanh, Martin Luther King, Jr., Florence Nightingale, Thomas Merton, Abraham Lincoln, the Dalai Lama, Nelson Mandela, Henry David Thoreau, Sister Wendy Beckett, Buddha, the poet Mary Oliver, and even the televised painter Bob Ross.

Instead of aspiring to imperfect and uninformed imitations, we might, more realistically, consider taking time to learn about any individual and seek to understand how someone faced and overcame circumstances or struggles, attained progress or inspired change, and succeeded in some manner without crumbling entirely or succumbing to temptations of vanity, domination, desire, or self-importance. With that kind of foundational knowledge, we may stand a much better chance of gaining insights and inspiration from their examples.

So, we don't really have to "be Socrates" or attempt to match his interrogative maximum in order to become advocates for education and objective truth. Anyone has the potential to examine things more logically and empirically, to exercise reason more diligently, to refuse perpetuating misrepresentations, to refute misconceptions, and to be more attentive, dispassionate, and balanced when handling facts. We could always start by being more honest with others and ourselves, admitting more readily when we do not know or when we are incorrect.

Each of us can develop our critical thinking skills and use them more conscientiously to evaluate information we encounter, along with its origins and agendas. We can approach these responsibilities individually, or as communities, or as generations sharing in the collective interests of more accurate knowledge, existential betterment, impartial justice, unconditional equality, merciful liberty, tolerance, kindness, humility, and voluntary peace.

To look at this another way, the proverbial "better world" most of us would gladly have realized in our lifetimes seems least likely to arrive through increased ignorance, desolation, injustice, inequality, oppression, prejudice, cruelty, hubris, or devastation.

We could attempt, with confidence, daring achievements and not let ourselves lapse into arrogance or vanity. We can conduct ourselves with both determination and open-mindedness. We can be fearless as well as humble throughout all our proceedings. None of these things are contradictory or mutually exclusive. We could look back at Socrates and move ahead, beyond the vicious circles of ancient debates, resolved to learn enough from the past so we could frame and phrase the first of many fateful questions, which, in the future, may move us, and our world, closer to the redemptive answers and serenity of enlightenment.

ESSAY II: THE VICARIUM

In my poem "Vicarium," the narrator recognizes the difficulties of trying to understand another person and reaches a profound conclusion:

> I must be you and not your things,
> espouse your atoms to the last,
>
> absorb your stories, live your past,
> breathe in your voice, dismiss myself,
> endure your scars, your every choice,
> envelop nothing but the whole
> if I presume to know your soul.

This poem offers an example of what I call *entering the Vicarium*, which I'll try to define as follows:

> "to contemplate life vicariously through the perspective of another person, location, idea, or object – all with the hope of gaining a clearer and deeper understanding of that someone, somewhere, or something."

The Vicarium establishes a *contemplative mode of observation* through a *perspectival point of study* with awareness, altruism, empathy, and tolerance as its primary motivations when it involves persons or ideas. Through this meditative vantage point, contemplators have the potential of gaining numerous insights into other persons or things.

The word "Vicarium" is inspired by the word *vicarious*, the adjective we use when describing *experiences witnessed through another person*, as when we see someone crying or laughing: on some level, we may start to consider that person's emotional state or pain, whatever that person is experiencing or might have gone through, and we might then share in that feeling and begin to empathize.

Among *ideas*, *things* and *places*, the Vicarium has the potential of inspiring new thinking, metaphors, and realizations. Imagine experiencing the endless dynamics of life and motion as an ocean – whales cruising beneath or seagulls soaring above while ships of all sizes drift in and out of view and the sky cycles between blazing sunlight and twinkling stars.

Technology enthusiasts might wonder, "Can't we already do that?" Of course, these days, someone can wear a virtual reality (VR) viewer and stand virtually anywhere inside of computer-generated environments. VR is a user-centric, visual (and sometimes haptic) perception-based medium reliant on and created by technology.

There's also "augmented reality" (AR), which, through a digital viewer like a computer tablet, can superimpose information (such as walking or driving directions, names and hours of businesses, or contact information) over live video feeds based on what someone films (with their digital devices) and where that person physically stands.

The Vicarium transcends perception and has nothing to do with technology. Someone (the *considerer*), who *enters the Vicarium*, becomes the contemplative observer vicariously witnessing life through the perspective of the other person, location, idea, or object (the *considered*).

Also, the *considered* can be anywhere, from any point in time – past, present, or future – and be real or imagined, such as a historical figure or a literary character, who can be "observed" respectively through biographical information or a literary text.

With an open mind, the Vicarium could be a creative or educational tool that has some potential of teaching us more about ourselves, each other, and all that surrounds us, physically and conceptually. How wonderful it would be if our capacities for tolerance, compassion, equality, and justice could increase as we engage more viewpoints, enter more regularly into the experiences of others, and extend our awareness and our concerns well beyond ourselves.

Many of us have already been doing some of these things subconsciously as readers who tend to think at length about a character's actions, words, situations, or decisions. Any use of the Vicarium might also benefit from insights and alternate perspectives we've reached through our reading experiences and our interpretive abilities.

Literary scholars and critics have often served as formal *considerers*, contemplating key characters, ideas, and storylines, and sometimes even comparing those observations with archetypes, mythological figures, or similar characters and plot points found in other literary texts. Such observational and interpretive scholarship occupies entire databases and ranges of bookshelves, especially in academic libraries, but the Vicarium is not limited to scholars: it is available to anyone.

Imagine how many amazing insights any one of us may have the potential to witness with just a little more awareness and consideration.

ESSAY III: ACCESSIBLE ME

I believe I was around seven years old when my mother gave me an anthology of classic poetry – a significant gift which would set me on the aspirational path to becoming a poet. Many of those poems went right over my head at that age, but I *liked* that. I wanted to figure them out. I worked at them, line by line sometimes, trying to unearth meanings as an archaeologist might dig through earth for artifacts.

In high school, and then as an English Literature major in college, I'd meet with far more difficult poetry. Words, imagery, allusions, and symbols could be researched and deciphered eventually, but there were more abstract or emotional things which could resist complete comprehension, especially in some free-flowing or intensely personal poems which offered little context and could have meant any number of things when I was anticipating something clearer or more definite.

That kind of difficulty mostly reflected my inexperience with such styles, themes, and situations. Maturation helps, as does increased reading, traversing the world, living life, getting more inquisitive, exercising imagination, and considering things from new perspectives. Some poems and literary works can have phrasing or constructions that resist immediate understanding or may seem unfamiliar or unconcerned with being understood.

I've met some poems who guard their secrets very well or aren't especially forthcoming, and that's just fine: poetry *is* part of a spectrum of expression which welcomes for all conceivable possibilities, including the seemingly impossible or the illegible. Each poet makes choices for reasons we may never wholly grasp. I completely respect that and recognize how rich and varied those choices help to make the geography of poetry's world wonderfully varied and fascinating. How tedious it would be if everyone wrote the same, and utterly plainly so, in a verbal flatland of vapid verse.

As I approached college, writers like Dante, Eliot, Milton, Pound, and Joyce were towering literary figures I regarded highly. I admired the depths and complexity their poetry achieved, and I eventually allowed myself to dream of producing works aspiring to the literary intricacies of *The Divine Comedy*, *Paradise Lost*, *The Waste Land*, *The Cantos*, *Ulysses*, and even the prose but poetic *Finnegans Wake*.

I started writing difficult poems, weaving complexities with tinges of elevated diction and worldliness but little actual meaning. I even wrote an excessively epic poem (*Lines*) that ran over a hundred pages. These attempts were ridiculously forbidding and impractical constructions. As their architect, I managed to design them with almost no windows and entrances, and their properties were surrounded by imposing fences or impassable boundaries. They were inaccessible. Thankfully, that was a brief phase, and I would choose a different path.

My "sophomoric" poetry submissions saw more rejections than my "freshman" works, and deservedly so (yes, I can say that now). A few times I shared some of my "difficult poems" with some schoolmates and professors. Instead of the kind of compliments I received for some of my earlier poems, I met with blank looks, fake smiles, and questions. Nearly no one really understood what was being expressed or cared to think too long about that. Someone actually quizzed me on the spot, pointing to a stanza, asking what I was trying to say there.

I'm grateful for those reactions: they helped me realize I *did* want to be understood, mostly. I didn't want to purge my works of profound thoughts and elevated diction, but I also didn't want my readers to feel perplexed, irrelevant, or unwelcome. On the yards of my poems, I didn't want any "Keep Out" or "No Trespassers" signs posted. What I did want was for anyone to feel they could approach and enter a poem of mine as if it were an open house, a place where they could feel completely at home, walk around, sit, stay a while, and enjoy the conversation or the views. I decided I wanted to be more accessible.

If felt like I made a major career choice back then, and it really was. My personal decision to be a more accessible poet is mine alone. Not for a single moment do I mean to suggest or imply that it is the "correct" or preferred mode for anyone else. All authors and artists must decide how to approach their expressions. As for myself, I refuse to believe in a "right" or "wrong" kind of poetry. I believe we need poetry, art, and music of every kind (see my poem "Art of Diversity"), and that diversity belongs everywhere, in and beyond all modes of human expression.

To me, *accessible* simply means *your writing can be understood with little or no effort on the reader's part*. I see nothing negative or limiting about the word or its antonym *inaccessible*, which I tend to see as most often meaning *your writing is challenging but it has the potential of being understood with effort and/or additional information*. I know that some people might use *accessible* in a pejorative sense, suggesting a writer might be derided for being *too open, too easy to read, too clearly expressed*. Just as I do not assume *inaccessibility* means *completely unintelligible*, I do not perceive *accessibility* as necessarily oversimplifying ideas and diction or refraining from challenging or inventive stylistic or structural decisions in any literary work.

There's always more to consider. How meaning is or is not conveyed is something we cannot afford to ignore as writers, I think. The likelihood of someone understanding anything we express already depends on lingual, cognitive, and other variables no one can completely prepare for or control. And then there are interpretations, misconceptions, assumptions, biases, incomplete knowledge, distracted thoughts, and the unpredictable happenings of life itself. Anyone's probability of being understood can vary substantially at any hour.

I especially admire writers who can face all those unknowns and still find compelling ways to assemble words in uncommon combinations, creating something uniquely beautiful yet ultimately understandable, despite any unusualness. E. E. Cummings did that quite a bit in his verbally and typographically inventive poetry. In his poems, syntax could somersault, and letters themselves could ice-skate around the printed page. Yet, for all his acrobatics, Cummings' poetry never leaped completely into the chasm of the obscure.

Literature offers many notable examples of such talent. William Shakespeare, perhaps our most classic and surprising example of accessibility, wrote poetry and dramas in an earlier form of English. Shakespeare made full use of the language of his day and is credited, to various degrees by various scholars, as having coined words still used today. He wrote most poetically, made many allusions and mythological references, concocted complex characters, and wove intricate plots and subplots. Still, he engaged *all the audience,* not merely the elite theatergoers.

Our initial inability to understand Shakespeare often has much to do with the stylistic differences of English between now and then. Annotated texts and modern translations can help readers with that, and there are no shortage of summaries and studies of his works. Shakespeare's works live on and continue to be quoted centuries since their composition because their stories and meanings related with audiences and resonated clearly and far, in distance and years. It is no accident that neither the evolution of the English language nor time itself could render Shakespeare unreadable, indecipherable, or irrelevant: his word choices and stylistic decisions ensured his works would remain understandable and enjoyable for a very long time.

Longevity of legibility is a truly remarkable achievement when we consider how languages (and dialects of those languages) continue to evolve. New words and phrases arrive regularly while some words – or entire languages – near extinction due to non-usage. Surviving words accumulate additional meanings and can become entwined with other words, contexts, word parts (e.g. prefixes and suffixes), and connotations, which other generations of readers may overlook, misinterpret, misuse, or redefine.

And then there is the matter of translation and transliteration: the painstaking challenge of making a literary text readable in another language without losing the meaning and verbal beauty of the original work. No two languages are the same, and their grammatical and semantic differences only increase the translator's difficulty of word choice. Chronologies and colloquialisms make the task even more formidable. Despite these many variables, some steadiness of meaning survives each century, and literary works written decades to millennia ago may still speak to us and disclose things we did not know.

Much of that has to do with the clarity and quality of writing those authors achieved. On the far end of the expressive spectrum, we have James Joyce's *Finnegans Wake*, perhaps literature's most famous example of *inaccessibility*. It is a stupendous work that survives as a literary rarity, a product of genius, however challenging it may be for various readers. Its daunting nature is, for some people, central to its appeal. To have read it entirely *is* an achievement (one I cannot claim for myself yet, although, someday, I do hope to make it all the way through).

Still, I admire Joyce's adventurous choices as an author, particularly in his novel *Ulysses*, which he modeled after Homer's *Odyssey*. Compared with *Finnegans Wake*, *Ulysses* is a very accessible text, even with its most remarkable conclusion – a "stream of consciousness" (flowing thoughts) exceeding 20,000 words voicing every last fleeting whim gushing from Molly Bloom's wandering and ecstatic mind as she reclines and muses famously about life and love. Bravo to Joyce for having the nerve and sheer talent to push the envelope so far.

I could never compete with that, nor would I be inclined to try. There are countless other ways we can express things creatively and captivate readers. These days, I'm more concerned how anything I express can affect the clarity, enjoyability, and survivability of my writing. I know the solution is not to avoid or ignore difficult ideas or styles. I have found it best for me to defer to the poem itself: honoring whatever it wants to think, however it wishes to speak, and wherever it wants to go.

Most of the "persona poems" I write often develop their own voices and will at some early point in their creation. As that happens, I try to listen to them more carefully, even when I don't always agree entirely with what they're saying or where they're going. This might sound funny, but it's really not much different than the characterization and dialogue storytellers will use to develop their own plays and novels. Dramatists and novelists rarely create characters based on their own mirror images. What an exercise in vanity that would be. Poems can possess their own identities which are fully distinct from the poet's personality.

Consider the many voices – over 200 of them – in *Spoon River Anthology* by Edgar Lee Masters, all speaking from the hereafter: such a unique poetic work of personal and interrelated narratives would not be possible had the poet imposed his own disposition and voice over theirs. Sure, some characters in literary works can have trace traits of the author in them, but writers who wish or need to engage readers so directly could quit the act, forego costumes, step out from behind the curtain, and deliver a speech directly to the audience without any pretense.

This is why I would suggest that, while the voice of Prufrock might resemble Eliot's, he is not Eliot entirely, just as the Duke is not really Browning, Lady Lazarus is not completely Plath, and the Siren is someone other than Atwood. And likewise with Hamlet, Lear, Falstaff, Prospero, or Puck: they are not Shakespeare. They were conceived in poetry but they have emerged distinctly with wits, emotions, and souls of their own, upstaging their own stories to become as if alive – so much so that they've transcended fictionality, become larger than life, and are now, so many years later, familiar to many people who never even attended their respective plays.

Shakespeare's success, in part, has persuaded me to believe "being accessible" doesn't always mean I have to give up any artistic, verbal, or psychological sophistication in my work. On the other side of the matter, Joyce has also helped me to appreciate the full extent of literature's expressive spectrum, and his writing shows it is possible for writers to go further than expected and still be acclaimed for their courage and innovation.

Far better poets than me have proved it is feasible to achieve eloquence, profundity, and accessibility *all at once.* Many excellent examples abound in the plainspoken yet potent poetry of Billy Collins, Mary Oliver, Walt Whitman, Emily Dickinson, Robert Frost, William Carlos Williams, and others. These exceptional writers show, beyond any doubt, literary creations can be hailed in multiple respects: for their beauty and their functionality, their eclecticism and their newness, their modesty and their grandeur, as well as their complexity and their clarity.

Whenever I recall all of these things have become possible and then real for other writers, I resume my own journey as a poet with renewed hope, a stronger sense of direction, and a much clearer awareness of how far I have yet to travel.

POETRY WORDS: A VERY BRIEF GLOSSARY

It's always my hope more people will choose to make poetry a permanent part of their lives. I believe that could happen if more folks find out there's plenty of poetry that's accessible and readily appreciable.

If anyone is curious and feels like learning a little more about poetry, I'm including this simple little glossary. Honestly, you don't need to know any of these terms in order to enjoy a poem. You can skip this section, if you wish.

My definitions below aren't of any academic quality, nor are they meant to be. There are entire books by better authors and more knowledgeable scholars who can define these things comprehensively.

If you're interested in that level of information, I've included some of those titles in the next section of recommended poetry books.

Words about Sounds in a Poem

Alliteration: Words near each other that start with similar sounds. Examples: *beautiful butterflies, sparkling stars, roaring rivers, majestic mountains.*

Assonance: Words repeating vowel sounds. Examples: the letter O in *flowing ocean*, the letter A in *famous places*, the letter E in *endless meditations.*

Cadence: The rhythmic roll of words.

Consonance: Words repeating consonant sounds. Examples: the letter S in *distant stars across the cosmos*, and the letter N in *hidden entrance.*

Meter: When words in a poem flow in mostly repeating rhythmic patterns of emphasis (stressed or unstressed syllables) line after line, meter is present.

Onomatopoeia: Words that sound like what they describe. Examples: *hum, fizz, splash, click, whoosh.*

Rhymes: Words ending in similar or identical ways. Examples of rhyming words: *sight* and *light, sigh* and *fly, see* and *free.*

Words Describing Some Kinds of Poems

Concrete Poem: A poem that can use creative letter and word placement, spacing, along with stylistic lettering (typography), or shapes to express something. For example, a poem about someone might take the shape of a face.

Dramatic Monologue: A poem narrated by a character. Sometimes called a *persona poem*. T. S. Eliot's poem "The Love Song of J. Alfred Prufrock" is one of the best examples of this kind of poem.

Ekphrastic Poem: A poem about or inspired by art. One example in this collection is my poem "To a Praying Sculpture."

Elegy: A poem about death or someone who died.

Epic Poem: A long poem that tells a complex story mainly focusing on a heroic character. Homer, an ancient Greek poet, is famous for having created the epic poems *Iliad* and *Odyssey*.

Haiku: A Japanese form of poetry, and one of the shortest, most popular kinds of poems around the world. Traditional haiku focuses mostly on nature. Despite its compact form, a haiku poem can be very expressive and profound.

Lyric Poem: A compact personal poem expressing thoughts, memories, or emotions.

Ode: A poem of praise, or honoring, or celebration, often elevated in tone while addressing or describing the person, place, or thing being revered.

Sonnet: A classic poetic form popularized by William Shakespeare and others. Traditional sonnets have fourteen lines and a set pattern of rhymes (rhyme scheme).

Words about a Poem's Structure

Form: Poetry exists in many "forms," such as haiku or sonnets. Poetry forms have rules for specific things in a poem, such as how many lines a poem contains, how the poem is structured, or which lines in the poem should rhyme with each other.

Free Verse: Poetry that's free of the constraints of poetry forms, rhymes, and rhythms. Free verse can have irregular rhythms and resemble regular speech.

Line: In a poem, it's one or more words in a row. Lines can be long or short, sometimes extending beyond the margin of a printed page and then wrapping around to the other side. There's even such a thing as a one-line poem. When, in a line, words continue (without a pause at the end of the line) into the following line, we call that *enjambment*. A technical consideration worth mentioning: when you read a poetry e-book, longer lines in a poem can wrap around the screen's margins in ways a poet never intended; that's *not* enjambment, just the side-effect of a computer trying to fit words on a screen.

Lineation: How a poem's words get arranged into lines of text.

Rhyme Scheme: The regular or formulaic arrangement of rhymes in a poem. Different poetic forms, such as the sonnet (and certain kinds of sonnets), require different lines to rhyme with each other. Many kinds of poems, such as *haiku* or *free verse*, don't rhyme.

Stanza: One or more lines of text grouped together in a poem. It's comparable to the paragraph in regular writing. An empty vertical space separates one stanza from another.

A Few Other Words

Allusion: A reference made to something else, such as another poem or literary work, a name or character or place (real, fictional, or mythological), a symbol, a piece of music or work of art, or a word, phrase, or quote. Allusions establish connections with these other works and things, which also might allude to other works and things, which also – well, you get the point. Good allusions aren't just cameos or name-drops: they establish purposeful connections that can increase or enhance the meaning, context, and interpretive potential of a literary work.

Apostrophe: When something that's not alive (or someone who's not around) is being addressed by a narrator or the poet. Examples of this technique can be found in some of the poems in this book (e.g. "To Tolkien, the Mythmaker" and "Metropolis").

Diction: The kind of words used in writing. Classic poems, such as the sonnets of William Shakespeare, often resonate with more formal or verbally extravagant voices than what we usually read or hear in daily speech or today's writings. The diction in many contemporary poems can sound more modern, conversational, and personal.

Etymology: The history of a word and the meaning of its various parts, such as its prefix or suffix. Some dictionaries include etymologies along with one or more usage examples showing how that word has been or can be employed.

Imagery (or **Images**): Things ("images") mentioned or described in a poem. For example, a poem about a garden might mention or describe flowers and butterflies. Sometimes an image functions as a symbol.

Interpretation: What a reader or listener *thinks* a poem could mean, or how a poet portrays something through words. As a reader, when you "interpret a poem," you're attempting to understand what's going on in a poem: what it *seems* to say, based on its words, imagery, metaphor(s), etc., and then perhaps what it might *also* mean from *another* perspective, after you reconsider everything. All writers, artists, and performers interpret ideas in their chosen media and create things that are "open to interpretation" in various ways. Interpretation enriches human expression with imagination as well as new potential contexts, comparisons, meanings, and questions.

Metaphor: Equating one thing with another, as in the line "You press on my piano heart" from my poem "Emblazon," where the narrator equates the heart with a musical instrument. Metaphors let us explore potential connections between two seemingly different things. Beyond inspiring creative thinking, metaphors can help us discover shared qualities, apparent parallels, and deeper relationships between persons, places, things, or ideas.

Perspective: A position from where you see or understand something. We each see things, physically or mentally, from different points. We're all unique thanks to our diversity, and that uniqueness can help us see and understand things in various ways. Through reading and writing poetry, we can explore and express endless perspectives, witnessing things through someone else's position and possibly learning more about our lives.

Simile: A metaphor says "[insert object A here]" is "[insert object B here]," while a simile says "A is like B," as in these lines from my poem "Tao": "the universe / unfolds and thrives / just like the lotus." A metaphor equates things, whereas a simile compares.

Speaker: The narrator or voice of the poem. In some poems, it could be a character who is either anonymous or identified.

Sometimes it can be an object or a place that speaks to us as if it were alive. In other poems, it could be the poet directly addressing the audience. It's never safe to presume the poet is the narrator. For example, I engage different perspectives and voices throughout my poems and will write from their variously imagined personalities (personas).

Symbol: Something that can represent or suggest another thing. Some symbols carry a number of meanings. For example, the U.S. flag represents the country, but it can also mean "democracy" or "freedom" or something else to different persons. Symbols can be visual, described, artistic, spiritual, mathematical, mythological, governmental, scientific, or something else. Poets and readers can interpret certain symbols uniquely.

Zenith: Not a standard literary term, but something I sometimes use when describing a "high point" of anything expressed in or beyond poetry. An example of a "high point" could be a word, phrase, image, or idea that stands out, or it could be the most meaningful or memorable part or aspect of a poem (or any form of expression). Applied to music, it could be the most moving or memorable part of a song (e.g. a guitar riff or a drum solo).

"Climax" is a standard term used to describe the turning point or peak point of conflict, and then resolution, in a traditional storyline, where conflict builds intensely until resolution. A zenith isn't always the climax: imagine a movie where a central character delivers an inspiring speech or does something you consider moving or remarkable.

Later in the story, there could be a struggle of some sort – perhaps even a full-blown battle – but, after the movie, what you tend to dwell on most of all is not the climactic combat but rather the more memorable "high point" of that character's speech or action.

Poetry tends not to be as sequential as stories, novels, plays, or screenplays, so the concept of a climactic storyline doesn't always apply to poems. Sometimes the ultimate "high point" in a poem is more subtle, less apparent – a phrase, a word, a thought, or a feeling.

In a sonnet, there is a "turning point" called the *volta*, where there's a sudden realization, or a notable shift of tone or thought, near the end of the poem. Sometimes the "high point" (zenith) could be that, or it could be something you encountered earlier, at the beginning even – in any kind of writing – a passage, stanza, or chapter that was exceptionally intriguing, profound, or so beautifully phrased that it stays with you.

SOME POETRY READING SUGGESTIONS

SOME BOOKS ABOUT POETRY

If you'd like to learn more about poetry, these are some books I recommend:

The Art of Poetry by Shira Wolosky
The Art of Reading Poetry by Harold Bloom
The Best Poems of the English Language edited by Harold Bloom
The Book of Forms: A Handbook of Poetics by Lewis Turco
A Book of Luminous Things: An International Anthology of Poetry edited by Czeslaw Milosz
The Discovery of Poetry by Frances Mayes
How to Read a Poem: And Fall in Love with Poetry by Edward Hirsch
How to Read Poetry Like a Professor by Thomas C. Foster
A Little Book on Form by Robert Hass
A Little History of Poetry by John Carey
The Making of a Poem: A Norton Anthology of Poetic Forms by Eavan Boland and Mark Strand
The Ode Less Travelled by Stephen Fry
Poemcrazy: Freeing Your Life with Words by Susan G. Wooldridge
The Poet's Companion by Kim Addonizio
A Poet's Glossary by Edward Hirsch
A Poetry Handbook by Mary Oliver
The Poetry Home Repair Manual by Ted Kooser
The Princeton Encyclopedia of Poetry and Poetics
A Primer for Poets and Readers of Poetry by Gregory Orr
Rhyme's Reason: A Guide to English Verse by John Hollander
Rules For the Dance by Mary Oliver

Singing School by Robert Pinsky

The Sounds of Poetry by Robert Pinsky

Ten Windows: How Great Poems Transform the World by Jane Hirshfield

Please also consider visiting your local library for even more poetry books.

SOME POETS YOU MIGHT LIKE

Here are some amazing poets I'd recommend to mature readers, including those who are new to poetry. For an expanded selection of poets, please see my next list.

Maya Angelou
Matsuo Basho
Wendell Berry
Elizabeth Bishop
Gwendolyn Brooks
Elizabeth Barret Browning
Lucille Clifton
Billy Collins
Emily Dickinson
Rita Dove
Robert Frost
Nikita Gill
Nikki Giovanni
Amanda Gorman
Joy Harjo
Langston Hughes
John Keats
Jane Kenyon
Ted Kooser
Philip Larkin
Denise Levertov
Ada Limon
Amanda Lovelace
Amy Lowell
W. S. Merwin
Edna St. Vincent Millay

Pablo Neruda
Sharon Olds
Mary Oliver
Robert Pinsky
Christina Rossetti
Rumi
Kay Ryan
Charles Simic
Tracy K. Smith
Natasha Trethewey
Alice Walker
Walt Whitman
William Carlos Williams
William Wordsworth

ADDITIONAL POETS YOU MIGHT CONSIDER

The following alphabetized list represents additional poets I'd recommend to mature readers who believe they are ready to dive into poetry's boundless ocean.

Poems by this diverse array of writers span the expressive spectrum, from the classic and the accessible to the contemporary and the occasionally unorthodox or challenging. All of these poets have produced distinctly phenomenal works worth exploring.

In the event you encounter a poem you don't quite understand, it just might not be the right time for it. Certain poems can make a lot more sense to us at different stages of our lives. When we revisit poems later on, we can discover things we missed before or even develop new insights and interpretations. So, please don't give up. Consider returning to that poem later on.

If you aren't sure where to start in this list, you might pick a poet at random and then look up that name either at your local library or on the Web. Later in this book I provide a select list of websites, such as Poets.org, where you can learn about many poets.

Chinua Achebe
Ai (Ai Ogawa)
Conrad Aiken
Anna Akhmatova
Elizabeth Alexander
Julia Alvarez
Yehuda Amichai

A. R. Ammons
Guillaume Apollinaire
Rae Armantrout
Matthew Arnold
John Ashbery
Margaret Atwood
W. H. Auden
Charles Baudelaire
Stephen Vincent Benet
Wendell Berry
Frank Bidart
William Blake
Richard Blanco
Robert Bly
Louise Boga
Eavan Boland
Anne Bradstreet
Joseph Brodsky
Rupert Brooke
Robert Browning
Charles Bukowski
Robert Burns
Lord Byron (George Gordon Byron)
C. P. Cavafy
Victoria Chang
Geoffrey Chaucer
Sandra Cisneros
Amy Clampitt
John Clare
Henri Cole
Samuel Taylor Coleridge
Hart Crane
Robert Creeley
E. E. Cummings
Dante (Dante Alighieri)
Ruben Dario

Walter De la Mare
Natalie Diaz
John Donne
Hilda Doolittle (H.D.)
Ian Doescher
Mark Doty
Paul Laurence Dunbar
Stephen Dunn
John Dryden
Du Fu
Carol Ann Duffy
Paul Laurence Dunbar
Mona Van Duyn
T. S. Eliot
Claudia Emerson
Ralph Waldo Emerson
Louise Erdrich
Lawrence Ferlinghetti
Carolyn Forche
Allen Ginsberg
Dana Gioia
Louise Gluck
Jorie Graham
Robert Graves
Linda Gregg
Marilyn Hacker
Hafez (or Hafiz)
Donald Hall
Robert Hass
Robert Hayden
Seamus Heaney
Anthony Hecht
George Herbert
Zbigniew Herbert
Juan Felipe Herrera
Jane Hirshfield

Homer
Gerard Manley Hopkins
Ted Hughes
Donald Justice
Bob Kaufman
Jane Kenyon
Jack Kerouac
Rupi Kaur
Galway Kinnell
Kenneth Koch
Yusef Komunyakaa
Maxine Kumin
Stanley Kunitz
Emma Lazarus
Edward Lear
Giacomo Leopardi
Li Po
Henry Wadsworth Longfellow
Federico Garcia Lorca
Audre Lorde
Richard Lovelace
Amy Lowell
Robert Lowell
Thomas Lux
Stephane Mallarme
Osip Mandelstam
Katherine Mansfield
Christopher Marlowe
Andrew Marvell
Edgar Lee Masters
Thomas Merton
John Milton
Mirabai
Marianne Moore
Paul Muldoon
Howard Nemerov

Naomi Shihab Nye
Frank O'Hara
Gregory Orr
Ovid
Wilfred Owen
Octavio Paz
Fernando Pessoa
Petrarch (Francesco Petrarca)
Marge Piercy
Sylvia Plath
Edgar Allan Poe
Marie Ponsot
Alexander Pope
Ezra Pound
Yung Pueblo
Alexander Pushkin
Kenneth Rexroth
Adrienne Rich
Rainer Maria Rilke
Arthur Rimbaud
Theodore Roethke
Mary Ruefle
Sonia Sanchez
Carl Sandburg
Sappho
James Schuyler
Sir Walter Scott
Robert W. Service
Diane Seuss
Anne Sexton
William Shakespeare
Ntozake Shange
Karl Shapiro
Percy Bysshe Shelley
Patricia Smith
Gary Snyder

Robert Southey
William Stafford
Gertrude Stein
Wallace Stevens
Mark Strand
May Swenson
Algernon Charles Swinburne
Wislawa Szymborska
Rabindranath Tagore
James Tate
Sara Teasdale
Alfred Tennyson
Dylan Thomas
Henry David Thoreau
Tomas Transtromer
Jean Valentine
Paul Valery
Paul Verlaine
Virgil
Derek Walcott
Phillis Wheatley
John Greenleaf Whittier
Richard Wilbur
Ella Wheeler Wilcox
C. K. Williams
Yvor Winters
Charles Wright
Judith Wright
William Butler Yeats
F. S. Yousaf
Kevin Young
Marya Zaturenska
Louis Zukofsky

This list is just the tip of the iceberg. So many more poets await your discovery! Please see my next section, Some Poetry Publications, for other places you can read works by many other poets.

SOME POETRY PUBLICATIONS

You can discover more poets through these and other poetry publications:

The American Poetry Review
The Antioch Review
Black Warrior Review
Chicago Review
Crazyhorse
Gettysburg Review
Granta
The Hudson Review
The Iowa Review
The Kenyon Review
New England Review
The Paris Review
Ploughshares
Poetry (popularly referenced as "Poetry Magazine")
Poets & Writers
Shenandoah
The Southern Review
The Threepenny Review
TriQuarterly
The Virginia Quarterly Review
The Yale Review

WEBSITES

My Links:

www.RobertJTiess.net
www.ArtOfInterpretation.com
www.twitter.com/robertjtiess

Some Poetry Websites to Explore:

Academy of American Poets
www.poets.org

The Library of Congress:
Poetry & the U.S. Poet Laureate
www.loc.gov/poetry

The Poetry Foundation
www.poetryfoundation.org

Poetry Society of America
www.poetrysociety.org

Poets & Writers
www.pw.org

ACKNOWLEDGEMENTS

The Humbling and Other Poems
by Robert J. Tiess © Copyright 2022

Front book cover image:
*"Socrates: Lessons for the Nescient, or
Semester's End at Raphael's School of Athens"*
by Robert J. Tiess © Copyright 2022

A very special *thank you* **to Sandra** for all your love, encouragement, and understanding while I prepared this book for publication. I am - and will always be - most grateful for you, my beautiful muse.

www.ingramcontent.com/pod-product-compliance
Lightning Source LLC
Chambersburg PA
CBHW060317050426
42449CB00011B/2529